WILTSHIRE FOLLIES

Jonathan Holt

AMBERLEY

Acknowledgements

I would like to thank the following landowners for allowing me access to their grounds to fully appreciate the artistry and skill used in creating the follies described in this book, and for permission to reproduce their photographs in this book: Rosaleen Mulji; Elizabeth Cartwright-Hignett; Amanda and Stephen Clark; Lady Weinstock; David Cornelius-Reid; Bryda Woodruff; Paul and Caroline Weiland; the Earl of Pembroke; John Robinson; Sir Henry Keswick; Penny Stirling and Colin Little; Francis Dineley; Lord Methuen; Bonnie and Stephen Morant; Michael Pitt-Rivers; Rory Guinness; Marlborough College; and Sandroyd School.

The Folly Fellowship

The Folly Fellowship is a registered charity dedicated to the preservation of the historical, architectural and constructional heritage existing in and around follies, grottoes and garden buildings for the benefit of the public. Any reader wishing to know more should visit the Fellowship's website at www.follies.org.uk or e-mail membership@follies.org.uk.

First published 2019

Amberley Publishing
The Hill, Stroud
Gloucestershire, GL5 4EP

www.amberley-books.com

Copyright © Jonathan Holt, 2019

The right of Jonathan Holt to be identified as the Author
of this work has been asserted in accordance with the
Copyrights, Designs and Patents Act 1988.

British Library Cataloguing in Publication Data.
A catalogue record for this book is available from the British Library.

ISBN 978 1 4456 8489 5 (print)
ISBN 978 1 4456 8490 1 (ebook)

Typesetting and Origination by Amberley Publishing.
Printed in Great Britain.

Contents

Introduction 4

Amesbury 5

Berwick St John 7

Bishopstrow 9

Bowden Hill 10

Bowood 11

Bradford-on-Avon 16

Bremhill 19

Castle Combe 21

Chedglow 22

Corsham Court 25

Devizes 28

Etchilhampton 31

Euridge 33

Fonthill 36

Grittleton 41

Iford 42

Lacock 48

Ludgershall 50

Marlborough 51

Melksham 54

Middle Woodford 55

Monkton Farleigh 57

Newton Toney 58

Oare 60

Salisbury 61

Seend 62

Stourhead 65

Swindon 75

Teffont Evias 77

Tollard Royal 78

Trowbridge 84

Wardour Castle 85

Westbury 88

Whiteparish 90

Wilton 92

Bibliography 96

Introduction

The history of architectural follies in Wiltshire reflects the cultural history of the county. The writers, politicians and businessmen of each period played their part in creating and commentating on the county's architecture, as well as the gardens and landscapes in which it sits. There's often a story behind the building of a folly, which is more than just artistic and technical skill, be it the use of the profits from industry, the spending of inherited wealth or the drive to express oneself. In practical terms, follies were built for purposes as diverse as viewing an estate or a hunt in progress, to signal to others, to show off wealth and to provide shelter and rest. These aims and sentiments have been evident from the sixteenth century and continue today, albeit in forms that have developed and changed over the years.

The major landowners included the Hoares of Stourhead, the Herberts of Wilton and the Lansdownes of Bowood, but often the county's follies are the works of common people, artisans who are forgotten or get no credit, or are women who lacked professional status but cut their style in a very individual way.

The prominent and most-read writers included John Aubrey and Celia Fiennes, while the most distinguished makers were James Wyatt, William Chambers, Capability Brown, John Nash and Isaac de Caus. But then there are more shadowy people like Joseph and Josiah Lane, simple grotto builders from Tisbury about whose personal lives we know little, but many of whose works can still be enjoyed today.

The style of follies has sometimes changed, sometimes stayed the same; sometimes they contain several styles, and are all the more extraordinary for it. Through reading about Wiltshire's follies, you gain insights into the characters and personalities of the county's residents. Like windows into their minds, these buildings are a way of comprehending the peoples' drives and motivations, whether they be megalomaniac, academic, profligate or creative.

If you have ever wondered why a particular odd or curious building was built, herein lies your answer, and this book will surely introduce you to some you did not know about. It's rarely a straightforward or routine sort of story; more likely it will be a tale of ingenuity, skill, flouting of convention and toil against the odds.

Jonathan Holt

Amesbury

OS Ref: SU 151418; Postcode: SP4 7EX

In 1772 Sir William Chambers was called in for advice by the Duchess of Queensberry concerning 'The Chinese House'. Born Lady Catherine Hyde, and marrying Charles, Duke of Queensberry, she was friends with the poet and playwright John Gay, who wrote a ballad about her:

> Thus Kitty beautiful and young
> And wild as colt untam'd
> Bespoke the Fair from whence she sprung
> With little rage inflam'd
> Inflam'd with rage at sad restraint
> Which wise mama ordained
> And surely vex'd to play the saint
> While wit and beauty reigned

While Chambers was considered the ideal architect for anything Chinese after he came back from China full of drawings and ideas for buildings, some of which he turned into reality, notably the Pagoda in Kew Gardens, the weight of evidence is against him realising anything at Amesbury. The correspondence between him and Kitty consists of only one letter, and there is no conclusive proof – such as drawings, plans or bills – to show that he did in fact execute the Chinese House.

There had been a temporary Chinese-style structure in the Queensberrys' garden but this disappeared, and writers such as Bishop Pococke noted the existence of a Chinese building at Amesbury for some time before Chambers was involved, but we cannot be sure whether they were writing about the temporary structure or the later one. As early as 1748 Daniel Defoe describes 'a Room after the Manner of the Chinese' in his *Tour thro' the Whole Island of Great Britain*. Then there is the painting believed to be by Oxford artist William Turner of the Chinese House, which looks nothing like the building we see today, having several rectangular windows rather than a single oval one. Turner lived from 1789 to 1862 – a period which would suggest that the building is much later than Chambers's potential involvement. Landscape historian Michael Cousins says that even if the attribution is incorrect, the style of the building is no earlier than the beginning of the nineteenth century.

One theory is that Chambers just gave advice about or finished off the existing structure, which is fed by the comment of the traveller and philanthropist Jonas Hanway in his *Journal of Eight Days Journey* (1757), in which he observes 'an humble imitation of a Chinese house which is well shaded and agreeable; but it consists only of one room, and is yet unfinished'. Chambers was often in the area of Amesbury, working on such curious houses as Longford Castle, and at Wilton, so it is most likely that he was called in to advise on a building that had been abandoned while the main house was completed.

What we see today is a very solid building that straddles a tributary of the Hampshire Avon. It is constructed of Chilmark stone and knapped local flint arranged in patterns, with deep projecting eaves and unglazed oval windows with sliding shutters and doors. A decorative frieze makes its way all around the building. The substructure has a square plan and is surrounded by a veranda with a fret balustrade and columns painted red, which dominate the building.

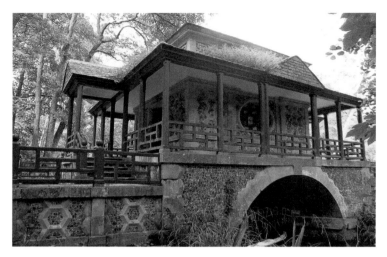

The Chinese pavilion at
Amesbury Abbey.

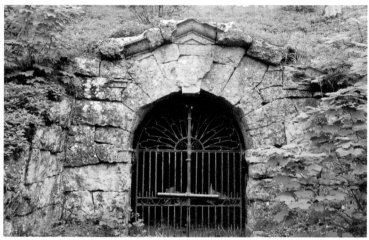

Gay's Cave.

The inner room may have been decorated. The Duchess was involved at every stage of the construction, and there is an extant letter from the Duchess to Chambers 'putting him in mind' of the work of a Swiss artist, Theodore de Bruyn, in order to 'elegantify' or 'embellish' the building, but not something 'intolerably tawdry'. Nothing remains of any decoration, so we cannot be certain that de Bruyn was involved. The estate accounts bear witness to a number of items of furniture which were bought for the summerhouse, including '1 small japand Tea-board' in keeping with the oriental style.

Charles Bridgeman landscaped the grounds with allées and triangles of plantings and clearings, as well as a quincunx, a curious configuration of slopes in the shape of a very large diamond. With a hint of an amphitheatre without the right shape to stage a play, its corners were once punctuated by statues. It was meant to be a kind of eyecatcher from the main house, being situated on the other side of the Avon at a distance of a couple of hundred metres. In the top of the quincunx, the Queensberrys built Gay's Cave in honour of their favourite playwright. This was a simple chamber set into the hillside with an arch beneath a groined vault leading to a curved back.

On either side was an unadorned niche. The curious aspect of its architecture is its massive stone façade, out of which just the pointed top of a pediment rises, and beneath are wrought iron gates. This was where Gay, so the story goes, is said to have written the words of the *Beggar's Opera*, but as the land was not acquired by the Queensberrys until 1734, two years after Gay's death, such stories are the stuff of legend. It has been attributed to Joseph Lane of Tisbury, but the only grounds for this idea are stylistic, and it lacks their seemingly haphazard style of construction. It was more likely designed by Henry Flitcroft, who worked at Amesbury for some thirty years.

Later owners, the Cornelius-Reids, had the Chinese Summerhouse rebuilt in 1986 after many years of neglect, and the Radley House Partnership won a Europa Nostra award for its restoration, in which they attempted to return the building to its original form, purporting to match the red paint to the original pigment found under later overpainting.

Berwick St John

OS Ref: ST 933243; Postcode: SP7 0EX

The desire to finish off a view, to embellish a landscape or to provide a viewing point is as strong today as it was in the heyday of the landscape garden. Continuing the tradition to the north of Berwick St John is Frances Dineley, an enterprising sheep farmer who has reused stone, mainly from the nearby demolished Ferne House, to first build the stables at his home Woodlands, and then much more romantic structures on his land. For example, the mock Gate House Belvedere has a mocking, dissimulating facet to it. While one stone has '1842' inscribed on it to suggest that this is a Gothic revival tower, nothing could be further from the truth. An indication of the playful nature of the man can be seen above the entrance to the flat roof where there is the Latin inscription 'NON SOLO MIHI LABORAVIT', which can be translated as 'Not only for myself have I worked', while opposite is 'SED SOLO LABORAVI' – 'But I have worked alone'. The latter is true, for this is very much a lone work, but for the benefit of all. It was not 'RESTORED 1979', as one stone inscription on the ground floor claims, but started in that year and it took ten years to complete. On the side of the tower there is a five-bar gate under an arch and an imposing crest, which was carved by Mr Dineley. He dismisses this as a simple task because the local Chilmark stone is so easily workable.

It was sited to be seen as an eyecatcher from the Banqueting Temple, which Mr Dineley started earlier in the 1970s and built of salvaged stone with Corinthian columns augmented by concrete lintels that he cast *in situ*, as well as a mainly wooden pediment. A central panel with the inscription 'FMD' declares that Francis Mark Dineley built it. Two doors on either side lead to a rear chamber, which was added around 2000 and is decorated finely with a ceiling depicting a blue sky and white clouds. Antlers surmount the fireplace and a simple medieval-style chandelier hangs from the ceiling. The inscription on the mantelpiece is another of Mr Dineley's declaration, and is closer to the truth this time:

PLURA INCOHAVI QUAM PERFECI SED PLURA EGO PERFECI QUAM ALII
INCOHAVERUNT
[I may not finish all that I start, but I start more things than most other people finish].

The sentiment is universal, for the one-man builder is often constrained by time and money in completing his work. Another folly he has been working on for a while is a small gazebo, a low stone tower in a wood behind the Banqueting Temple. As of 2017, it consisted of little more than one storey of breezeblocks, and what it might eventually look like is still firmly in Mr Dineley's very creative and enterprising head.

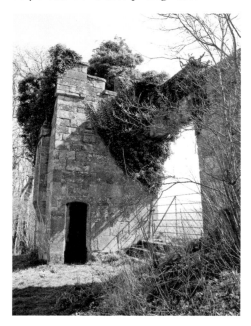

Left: The Sham Ruin.

Below: The Banqueting Temple.

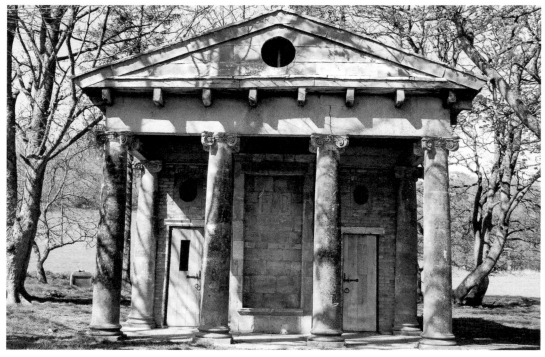

Bishopstrow

OS Ref: ST 896441; Postcode BA12 9HH

It's easy to like the situation of The Rotunda in the garden of Bishopstrow House near the end of a long, sweeping, rough lawn, which fits nicely into a small Arcadian landscape, but then you realise this small building is not well proportioned according to the best classical orders, having too high a dome for the eight relatively short columns. So it's not the best work of one K. Rogers, although you cannot fault the frieze with triglyphs running round its exterior. The inscription on the circular stone floor – 'Erected 1770' – tells us that it was built considerably earlier than the house, for that is the period from which this garden, situated to the east of Warminster, hails. It could have been cut off from the main garden when William Temple built his new house in 1817, but Temple was determined to have access to it by means of a tunnel under the Warminster to Salisbury road.

Temple's tunnel has a curved arch made of fine stone – some vermiculated, others smooth – with the incision of 'WT 1815' on both entrances. Once through, you can admire the rough lawns sloping down to the gently flowing River Wylye, which are well planted with yews, laurels and a large cedar, as well as a variety of deciduous trees. A small pavilion with two simple columns abuts a ha-ha and stands on a rise overlooking the river, its creeper partly taking over and adding to the character of this lovely scene. Over a fine iron bridge, the Vine House is overgrown by ivy, and there is a Venetian seat for the weary visitor, the seat itself a little weary in its fabric.

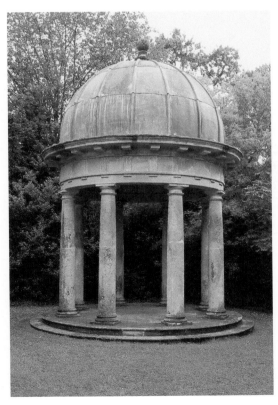

The Bishopstrow House temple.

Bowden Hill

OS Ref: ST 938682; Postcode: SN15 2PP

Around the same time that James Wyatt was completing the ashlar-faced south front of the main house of Bowden Park in 1796 for Barnard Dickinson, a sugar plantation owner and slave owner, the Grotto was also under construction. Its large bow window and four giant, unfluted Ionic columns are monumental when compared with the intimacy of the Grotto. While it has been claimed that the younger of the two master grotto builders of Tisbury, Josiah Lane, was its author due to similarities to his work elsewhere in Wiltshire, there is no proof.

It stands a couple of hundred metres from the house and faces a wide lawn, plane trees and a flower garden – a curiosity that has survived well thanks to some restoration. The similarities with the Lanes' work can be seen on the curved back of the structure with its rough stone – mainly tufa – scattered around. Serpentine passages take one through to the front, which has the type of façade not found on Lane's other creations: with no water flowing through, and none nearby either, it has the look of a summerhouse, featuring white-framed French windows with Gothic tracery and stained glass in the upper parts. Perhaps these features were added at a later date in order to enclose the Grotto, the main chamber being renovated by Stephen Bushell in 1987. Pendants of some fourteen ornamental crystalline stalactites decorate the ceiling, which is about 4 metres high, and the walls are encrusted with a wide variety of shells from nearby and far afield, as well as copper pyrites, quartz, coral and fossilised seaweed, all of which is laid out in random patterns. A band of ammonites set into the floor near the base of the wall is pale in comparison to the arrangement of tiles that radiate from a central agate. Fantasy is given full expression in this crystal cave, which glistens in the setting sun, for there is no need for candles until the last rays fade.

The floor has red and blue-black bricks, on which a photo board is habitually placed, showing the state of the Grotto during the course of restoration. This loss of elegance in the interior is compensated for by the charm of the exterior, with its creepers growing up towards its sloping, tiled roof. This is one of Wiltshire's largest decorated grottoes; massive in its conception, it is fine in its execution. Less remarkable is a standard rotunda, which is too far down in the grounds and too near bushes to form either an eyecatcher from the house or an obvious point of punctuation in the garden design.

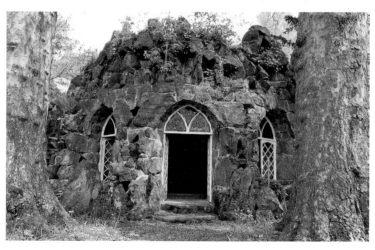

The Bowden Park Grotto.

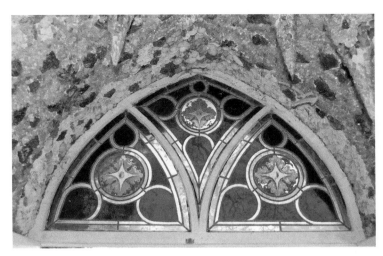

Bowden Park's stained glass window.

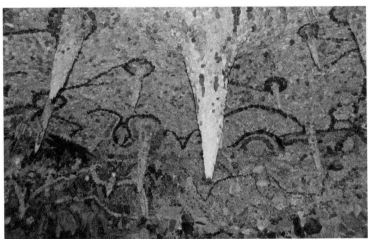

The stalactites of the Bowden Park Grotto.

Bowood

OS Ref: ST974699; Postcode: SN11 0LZ

> In this terrestrial elysium Nature has liberally dispensed her favours which her handmaid Art under the dominion of taste, has arranged and displayed in the most appropriate and becoming manner.

So wrote the Chippenham-born antiquary John Britton in *The Beauties of Wiltshire*, thinking highly enough of the Cascade to put the park at Bowood on the frontispiece of his survey of the county's picturesque sights. However, it is a flawed design, with few of the landscape features relating well to their surroundings. In themselves the features are undoubtedly fine, for the Mausoleum by Robert Adam is one of the most finely executed in any country park, the Cascade is a great rush of water and the expanse of the lake is an attractive, cooling heart to the park.

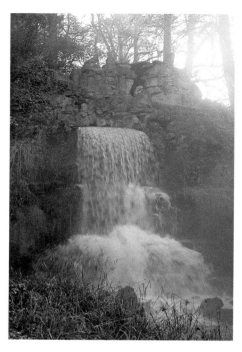

Bowood's Cascade.

The 1st Marquis of Lansdowne wished to create something similar to what Charles Hamilton had achieved on his estate of Painshill in Surrey. On the advice of Hamilton and with the inspiration of Poussin's paintings, Lansdowne set to work building the cascade in 1785. How far Hamilton played a part in the design is uncertain for there exists a plan at Bowood by John Whitehurst (1713–88) of Derby. His waterworks elsewhere were well executed and he was a prominent consultant in mechanics, pneumatics and hydraulics. His plan at Bowood appears to differ little, if at all, from the plan adopted, and so he must be given some credit for the cascade. It is also probable that he mastered the technical aspects. The builders appear to have been Williams Reeves and the family firm of Thomas King, both of Bath, with construction being completed in 1786.

With his father having worked on Hamilton's grotto at Painshill, it is accepted that Josiah Lane built the Grotto here. It is monumental in proportions and is more an extensive rockery with several tunnels. A 10-metre drop of water falls irregularly in roughly three stages, below which the water channels itself into a narrow stream in a dell, surrounded by a number of niches and copious vegetation. Josiah Lane built a zig-zag tunnel, curiously nicknamed the Crooked Mustard, which weaves its way about the top of the cascade, with plenty of niches, seats and little corners. After about 15 metres, one emerges into an open area, with massive, rough-hewn rocks scattered apparently haphazardly. Some 10 metres away, on the south side, is another large niche seating, from where one passes to more rockeries and seating. Britton was impressed:

> The dashing and the roar of the waters, jumbled confusion of the rock, the wildness and seclusion of the place, and various subterranean passages under the head of the river, conspire to render it a scene strikingly pleasing to every man of taste; but more peculiarly so to the painter and admirer of the picturesque; for here he may indulge himself in the reveries of fancy, and by a small effort of the imagination may think himself among the wild waterfalls of North Wales, or the thundering cataracts of Switzerland.

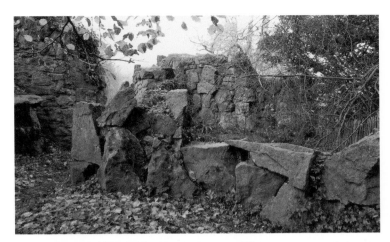

The Bowood Rockworks.

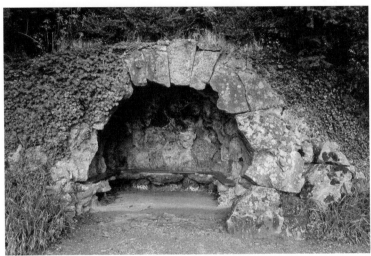

Bowood's Doric Temple.

Josiah Lane may also have been responsible for the simple Grotto or Hermit's Cave, the latter a recent appellation, overlooking the north end of the lake. Built around the same time as the cascade, this is an alcove with massive rockwork, an interior lined with tufa and a vault set with ammonites collected by the Reverend Townsend of Pewsey – a friend of the family and an eminent geologist who amassed Cornish ores and crystallisations. It has for the most part retained its encrustations and gives one an impression of how the cascade was once decorated.

On the east side of the lake is a plain, unremarkable tetrastyle Doric Temple, which was moved in 1864 to its present site from the Pleasure Grounds close to the house. Its architect is unknown and it may have been one of two temples. As an eyecatcher from the vicinity of the lake, it is adequate, but its positioning is typical of how Bowood misses its *genius loci* – indeed, it cannot be seen from the house or any other garden building, though it might have been visible from the house before the east wing was demolished in the 1950s. Capability Brown may have had something to do with this temple, for he visited Bowood as early as 1757 to negotiate with the first Marquis of Lansdowne, John Lord Shelburne.

The most impressive entrance to the estate is the Golden Gates, a major example of nineteenth-century British Italianate due to their fine ornamentation and authentic villa look. Designed in 1834–8 by Sir Charles Barry, who was also responsible for the Houses of Parliament, he had the 3rd Marquess' largesse to play with in gilding the very fine wrought iron, which includes some curves and swirls that pierce a crown. The structure consists of a triple gateway, one for carriages and two for pedestrians, and is flanked by a high campanile on one side and a small lantern on the other. Apart from the Ionic columns, the decoration lower down in the structure is more typically British, with armorial roundels including the Lansdowne motto 'VIRTUTE NON VERBIS' (virtue not words) as well as 'FAIRE UNIRE' (make unite), and a frieze with the Latin inscription 'PAX INTRANTIBUS ET HABITANTIBUS' (may you be at peace entering and remaining). Some fine sentiments!

To the south-west of the estate and set among the rhododendrons along Lady Shelburne's Walk is the Mausoleum, which was designed by Robert Adam in 1761–5. The living who wish to pay their respects enter by the ground-level door at the front; those who are dead enter by means of a sloping grass ramp at the back. Of ashlar stone, it is a square, domed building with classical elements, including Tuscan columns and a pediment with the coat of arms of the Shelburnes, who acquired the Lansdowne title later. The interior is fine too, with a delicately plastered ceiling and a number of niches and recesses with urns. At the far end stands a white sarcophagus by Carlini (*c.* 1775), with a long inscription remembering, as obsequiously as possible, the 1st Earl Shelburne, whose remains lie within. There is also a life-sized seated figure referred to as Mercury, but looking more female than male, by Alexander Brodie in 1862.

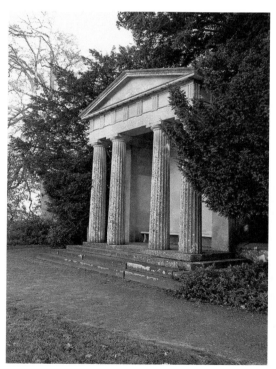 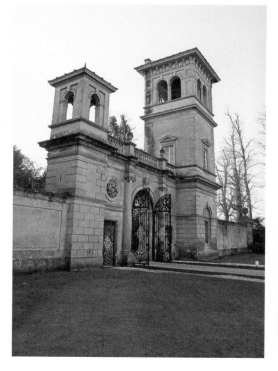

Above left: Bowood's Hermit's Cave.

Above right: The Golden Gates.

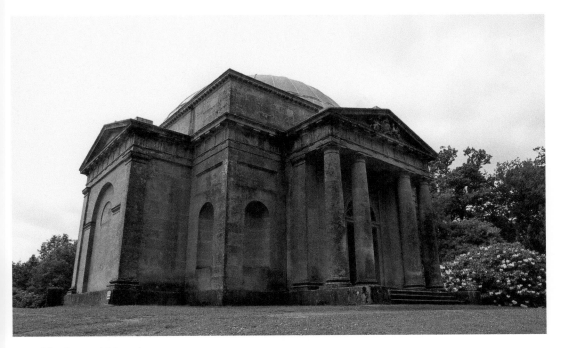

The Bowood Mausoleum.

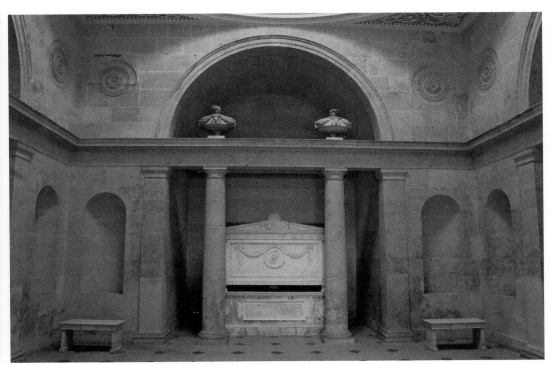

The interior of the Mausoleum.

Bradford-on-Avon

OS Ref: ST 815606; Postcode: BA15 1LZ

It is hard to do justice to the picturesqueness of Belcombe Court, an estate which goes back centuries and wears its beauty like a golden mantle. A perfectly proportioned seductress, it features some consummately executed ornaments, others of which have a raggedness about them. Here, John Wood the Elder extended the house substantially for wool merchant Francis Yerbury, and then set about decorating the grounds, some would say in a rococo way. It is likely that the almost kidney-shaped pond came first around 1730, but Wood did not design the Rotunda, and more's the pity for it does not have strictly classical proportions. He vented his displeasure in *An Essay Towards a Description of Bath* for Yerbury letting a local mason do it cheaper than Wood would have:

> … an error pardonable in the Working Mason to whom that part of the Pavilion was committed since he cannot be supposed to have ever heard of covered Monopterick edifices, much less to have known the Rules by which the Antients built them.

Wood makes no mention in his essay of the Grotto, which probably arrived around 1770 or 1780. On stylistic grounds, this was likely one of the several happy creations in Wiltshire of Josiah, the younger of the Lane father-and-son grotto-building team of Tisbury. The rough, natural, jutting up appearance, made with tufa or spongestone, is typical of the latter half the eighteenth century. It stands – as one might expect for a chamber which wishes to be dank – next to the pond, over which it has a view past a monolith that reputedly weighs 5 tons and supports part of the masonry above. It used to have mock stalactites, but these have mostly fallen, while the seats set into the walls remain. With two storeys, it boasts side passages below, through which one reaches a chamber with a floor made principally of ammonites and fossils. Reached by means of a flight of narrow steps is the upper level, known as the Banqueting Room, though it is open to the sky and more like a cramped belvedere. Much of the structure is enhanced by a fernery.

Since 1992 the estate has been owned by film director Paul Weiland, who has employed some of the best garden designers to embellish the grounds. Next to the west side of the house is the Shell

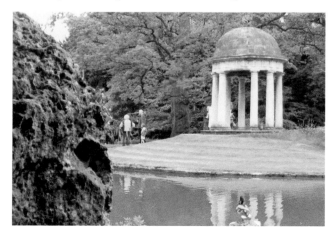

The Belcombe Court Grotto.

House, whose frame dates from 1891, featuring a pediment at the front containing a charming escutcheon in the shape of a peacock fanning out its feathers, and this is surmounted by a large curved gable reaching 16 feet. In the late twentieth century owner Bryda Woodruff created shell decorations, but these were removed and some of the shells were used by prominent shell artist Blott Kerr-Wilson, who has created something extraordinary. The most striking features are several circular swirls of shells, mainly white and also cream and blue with some pink colouring. The sides of the house are symmetrical, with the window frames covered in intricate designs. There is a thin frieze running around the upper part of the walls which cuts through the larger design. The minute complexity in the design is outstanding with a variety of shell embroidery including clams, mussels, scallops, periwinkles, oysters and a few cone and leopard exotics. The ceiling is of white scallops, the floor of pebbles. There are queen and spider conches over the west entrance, and the initials of the Weilands and their children are spelled out on the ceiling.

A Weaver's Cottage facing Wood's extension to the house forms part of the picturesque scene, as does a Rustic Gateway situated further up the hill and out of sight of the house. Made of limestone rubble, it has a rough lintel and quoins forming a large central archway, and again likely dates from Francis Yerbury's time. Further up and near the crest of the hill is the Gazebo, or Tuscan Temple – an oblong building with little embellishment apart from some stone seats. Essentially an eyecatcher, it is in a more fragile state than the rest of Belcombe Court, but it continues to be blessed by a caring owner and many admirers from far and wide.

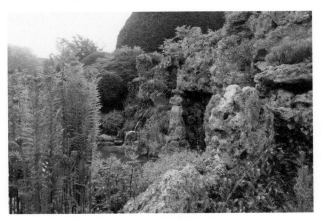

The Grotto.

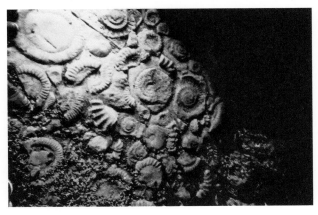

Ammonites in the Grotto.

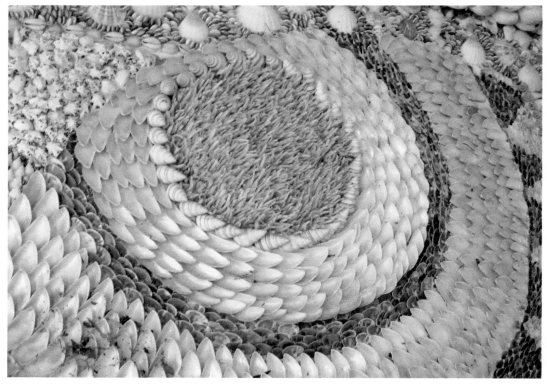

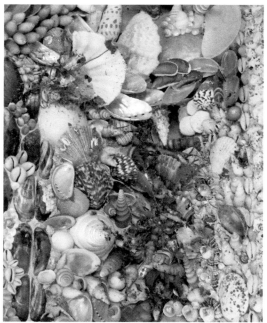

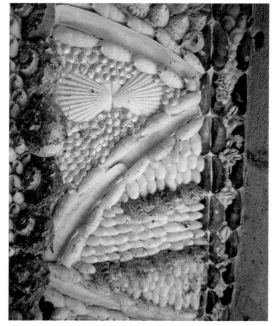

Decorations in the Shell House at Belcombe Court.

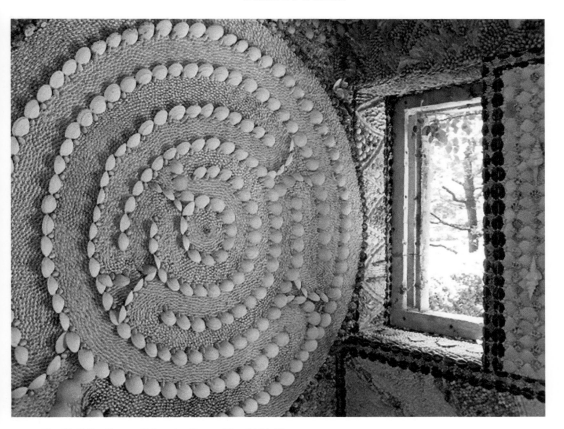

The Shell Pavilion at Belcombe Court. (Gerald Hull)

Bremhill

OS Ref: ST 973738; Postcode SN1 9LQ

According to Nikolaus Pevsner, Maud Heath was a 'very superior pedlar woman' who had more money than might be expected of woman of her class in the fifteenth century, and it remains a mystery to this day how she acquired it. She lived close to the River Avon between Calne and Chippenham, and while fed up with the mud that she had to wade through on the way to sell her wares at Chippenham Market, this issue was not rectified before her death in 1474. However, she had somehow managed to save enough money to leave a legacy of sufficient land and funds to build a raised causeway for pedestrians, as well as a parallel road for carriages totalling 4 miles in length across the frequently flooded marshes. £8 a year to maintain it was provided and a charity continued the upkeep and paid for the present bridge, at Kellaways, as late as the nineteenth century.

There are sixty-four arches in the causeway, at the start and finish of which a pillar with a ball top was erected to Maud Heath's memory in 1698. Eventually the local dignitaries felt that someone who had funded a road that had lasted more than three and a half centuries deserved more than a short ball-topped pillar. Something had to be done to preserve the memory of this good lady even further into the future, so in 1838 the Marquess of Lansdowne, whose nearby estate was Bowood, as well as the Vicar of Bremhill, William Lisle Bowles (1752–1850), put up a pillar, square in the lower half and hexagonal in the upper, crowned by the effigy of Ms Heath. Crudely executed and with no apparent attempt to flatter this unusual benefactress, she sits dumpily with a shopping basket in her left arm.

The Reverend Bowles was reputedly a 'frightened eccentric' according to Nicolaus Pevsner, and a poor poet who tried at Bremhill Court to copy the features of William Shenstone's Midland estate at the Leasowes. The Irish poet Thomas Moore was not impressed with his efforts, which 'had frittered away its beauty by grottoes, hermitages and Shenstonian inscriptions', but few survive. Bowles' friendship of other literary lights of his day, including Charles Lamb and William Wordsworth, did not prevent his inscription on the Maud Heath Monument being little better than doggerel, which hints at the fine views of North Wiltshire that can be seen, but misses no opportunity to preach:

> Thou, who dost on this aerial height,
> Where MAUD HEATHS Pathway winds in shade or light,
> Christian Wayfarer in a world of strife
> Be STILL, and ponder on the path of life
> W.L.B.

The other plaque erected by the road at the top of the hill says: 'From This Wick Hill Begins the Praise of Maud Heath's Gift to These Highways.' This is a place of simple beauty, embellished by a shaft of stone and a statue that complements the location.

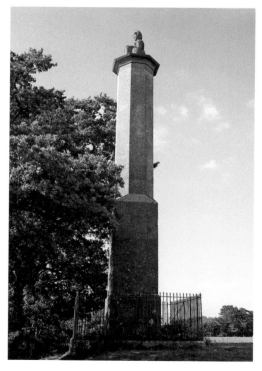

Maud Heath's Monument.

Castle Combe

OS Ref: ST 840772; Postcode SN14 7HR

The Manor House in the picture-postcard village of Castle Combe dates from 1664, but most of it is Victorian, with a new wing added in 1873 by Edward Chaddock Lowndes after he inherited in 1866. Lowndes took a great interest in the estate, and spent much of his fortune in the improvement of the manor property, employing Italians to add decorations to the ceilings and laying out the gardens with stonework and ornamental fountains.

Around 1884, Lowndes acquired the bell-turret and spire of the demolished Church of Saint Peter in Biddestone, a village a few miles away. It could be that various pieces were turned into ornamentation situated on a slope behind the house. These include the Fern House, situated at the top of a sloping garden, and leading from the Italian staircase there is a three-arched, now roofless gazebo. This features ornate arches and pinnacles that offer an ecclesiastical look, with a gentle bow shape at the front. Steps take you up to a terrace, inside which there is a pond with reeds. The sculpture of an armless half-boy, half-fish is set on a plinth of tufa. This stone continues on either side, forming part of the back wall and reaching a height of around a metre and a half. An ornate parapet runs between the pinnacles and roses climb up the pillars at the front of the arbour, while a yew hedge slightly obscures the view. Standing about 20 metres away are two curious seats capped by almost 5-metre spires, where one can stop for a break as one walks around the gardens. Are these other pieces of the former Saint Peter's? It's possible, judging by their ecclesiastical air.

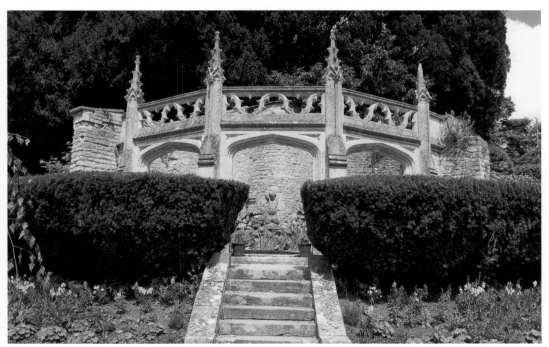

The Gazebo at Castle Combe Manor.

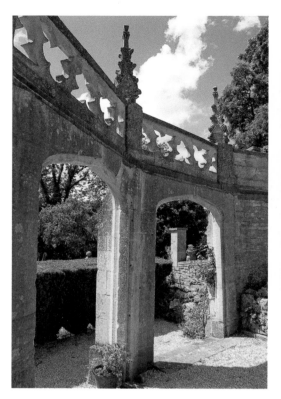
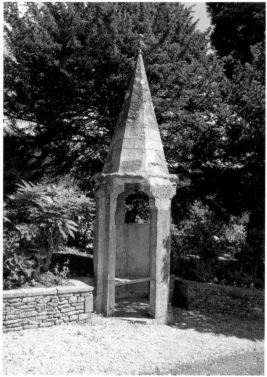

Above left: The Castle Combe Manor Gazebo from the rear.

Above right: The Pinnacled Seat at Castle Combe Manor.

There also used to be other towers set about the grounds, including the rest of the tower of Saint Peter's probably somewhere in the gardens. There were certainly two on the hill behind the manor – one lasting until 1950 and the other until 1962 – which were part of the castle built by the Scrope family in the Middle Ages.

Chedglow

OS Ref: ST 938926; Postcode: near SN16 9EZ

Little can prepare you for the sight of Colin's Barn, a construction of such originality and artistry that it takes your breath away. Built single-handedly by sheep farmer Colin Stokes, it is ostensibly a house for sheep, but it's much more than that: a series of embellishments take it to a different level than a simple sheep fold. The structure comprises dovecotes, turrets, arches and even one small room that is only accessible by crawling into an upper level – a difficult access that did not stop Stokes' ewe Beth from lying on his bed on more than one occasion in the room where Stokes stayed when his sheep were lambing, though he lived more normally in a cottage some 400 metres away.

Some 30 metres long and 10 metres deep, Colin's Barn is an extraordinary edifice that's the stuff of dreams. After buying the land in the 1980s, Colin Stokes started work in 1989 without a plan and minimal building experience, taking the honey-coloured Cotswold stone from his land while he farmed sheep in the area north of Malmesbury with the aim of building a store for hay and other supplies. He took inspiration from those buildings that he had seen during his life, and he wanted to build something that looked as if it belonged in its surroundings. He built solidly with great attention to detail, using bottles, plastic pots and any old containers to reinforce the walls and make air gaps in the concrete. The result is that while Colin's Barn may look remarkable, it

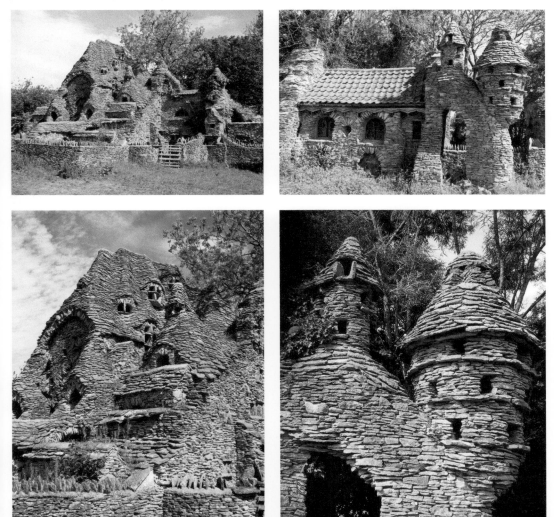

Colin's Barn.

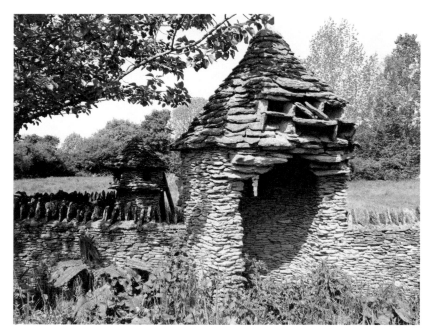

The Dovecot at
Colin's Barn.

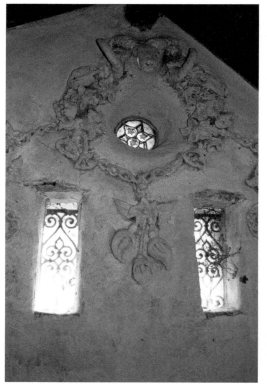

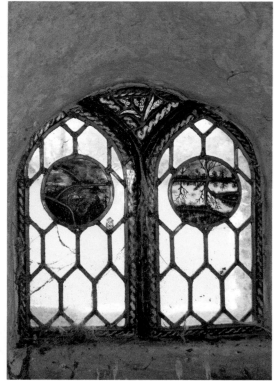

Above left and above right: The plasterwork and stained glass windows of Colin's Barn.

is not entirely out of place in the gentle, green, and slightly wooded Wiltshire countryside because of its use of local stone and features one might see in the neighbourhood.

It took him eleven years to build, until 2000 when he gave up due to the noise from a nearby quarry. He built bit by bit, starting small, laying all the stones up and pouring concrete down the back to secure it. Through one of the entrances to the barn is a spiral staircase that leads to the top of one of the dovecotes, which birds took over, including an owl that lived there the whole time he owned the land. A chapel-like separate building is used as a sheep shed. In the main barn, there is a yellow-painted main room, called the Hermitage, where a curved staircase leads to a niche. There are organic shapes such as leaves and flowers made of plaster, and several stained-glass windows that depict spring, summer, autumn and winter, as well as earth, air, fire and water, plus other references to the natural world. Beasts include a badger and a bird flying above the building, all hand-made by Stokes. Then, fairly suddenly, Stokes left to farm in Scotland.

Colin Stokes' philosophy can be expressed thus: 'A bit of skill comes in handy ... but you really need a sense of romance and a sense of humour. Anyone with so little sense of the ridiculous that they could look up "jabberwocky" in the dictionary and not be amused could never build a good folly.'

Corsham Court

OS Ref: ST 874706; Postcode: SN13 0BZ

Corsham Court has been the home of the Lords Methuen since 1745 and the present main house was built between 1844 and 1849 by Thomas Bellamy, a pupil of David Laing, a solid, but unremarkable piece of architecture created mainly out of Bath stone. Hellyer in the *Shell Guide to Gardens* conjectures that the same Bellamy also built the Folly Wall, a curious serpentine structure over 60 feet long and 30 feet high at its highest point. Roughly built, there is a bit of crenellation, a few chimneys and some genuine Gothic windows probably saved from a nearby church, perhaps Chippenham Abbey or Corsham Church, when the structures were either being demolished or restored respectively. Other features include a rectangular bellcote with a pointed main arch

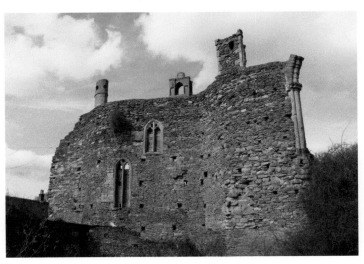

The Folly Wall.

flanked by panelled piers, smaller pointed arches on each side and a truncated short spirelet. There are two tiers of tall Gothic lancet windows. A sham coat of arms apparently dates it to 1874.

Is this a piece of 'the true rust of the Barons' Wars', a quality that Horace Walpole suggested that follies should have? Certainly it was used to screen the stables from the town of Corsham, and round the back there are a few lowly rooms for animal-housing purposes. Local legend says that either: a) Thomas Broadwood built the tall house in the street leading to Corsham Court and fashioned the wall so that he would not feel that the local 'Joneses' – the Methuens – had one up on him; or b) the Methuens wanted to maintain their superiority over upwardly mobile neighbours like Broadwood, who had built his daringly tall house within view of the Court, and they wanted to block out the view of his house. It is not likely that it was built by Humphry Repton, who landscaped at Corsham from 1799, finishing off the work of Capability Brown, who had produced a plan for the grounds dated 1761. Repton was more interested in creating something of lasting beauty. John Nash is said to have embellished the stables, so did he have a hand in the Folly Wall? It's not typical of his work, but the Bath House is.

Brown was the original designer of the Bath House. Arguably one of his finest garden buildings, it is satisfying in its style and neat in its proportions, and does not just follow a pattern book design like some of his other garden building. Built originally in around 1761–63, it has elements of the Elizabethan style, but these virtually disappeared beneath the Gothic when John Nash came to embellish it over five years from 1797 to 1802. It has a front open to the air, with a loggia of three arches, and inside the ceiling arches up to a point. The bath itself is oblong, being 6 feet wide by 12 long, and above there is a changing room. Light pours in through an ornate Gothic

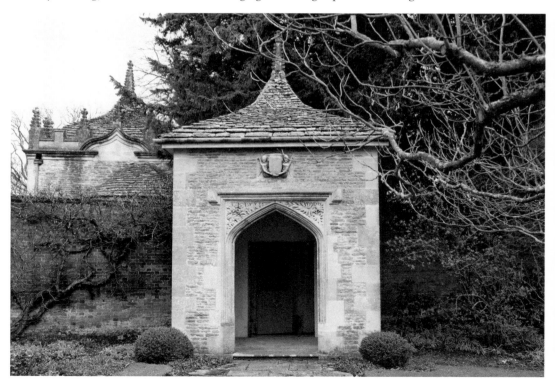

The Bradford Porch.

traced window with yellow and blue stained glass, either side of which are finely carved, if empty, niches. There also appears to be late medieval pieces of stone in the structure. The roof positively bristles with pinnacles.

And there is more to the Bath House than initially meets the eye. The innocuous-looking passageway leading towards the rear was originally entirely inlaid with fir cones and moss, and some of this decoration can still be distinguished. Carry on a little further and the surprise feature is at the end of the passageway: the Bradford Porch. This is a grand opening leading to the walled garden in the style of an arched, moulded Tudor doorway. A genuine late fifteenth-century fragment that had survived from the manor house at Bradford-on-Avon on its demolition in 1936, it includes a reused late medieval shield with two angel supporters and a fan vault with two stained glass shields inside.

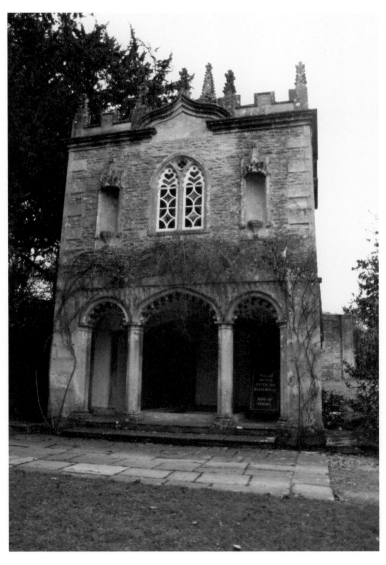

The Bath House.

Devizes

This most centrally situated town in Wiltshire has a number of buildings and monuments of interest that date from the nineteenth century and not further back in time as one of them may suggest. This is Devizes Castle (OS Ref: SU 002 613). It sits on a small hill situated more than a hundred metres from the market place that originally formed part of the outer bailey and is screened by high buildings and trees, so the connection between castle and town is diminished. What we see today is a Victorian re-imagining of a neo-Norman castle, complete with a bridge, if not a drawbridge, over a dried up and grassed over moat.

After demolition of the original castle, the latest additions were erected from 1842 by the prominent Bath architect and folly builder Henry Edmund Goodridge, who was responsible for the imposing Beckford's Tower in the famous spa city. The castle was given a new lease of life when the Leach family, local tradespeople, acquired it in 1838. Goodridge kept faith with the style of the original castle, adding a large, circular keep and battlements to the north tower, which was once used as a windmill, as was the south tower. Attached to the castle is the entrance called Saint John's Gate, which incorporates stonework from the nearby Saint John's Church.

The most remarkable addition is the Fernery – a curved Gothic room built by G. A. Randall under one of the round towers. This was a sort of ambulatory for long-gone lords and ladies of the manor, complete with fine traceried windows. The perimeter of the grounds is laid out with terrace walks which take the walker around a series of niches and gateways decorated more flamboyantly than was ever seen in Norman times, but echoing the styles of the times with zig-zag motifs and cable and billet mouldings.

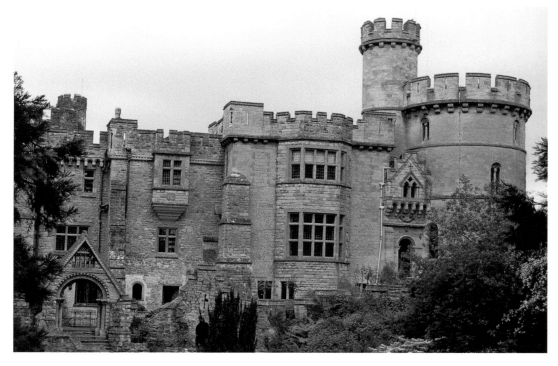

Devizes Castle.

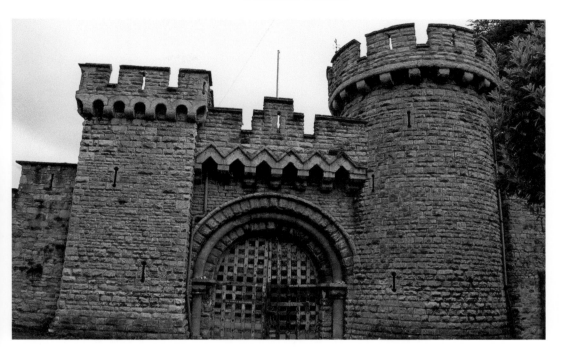

The Devizes Castle Gatehouse.

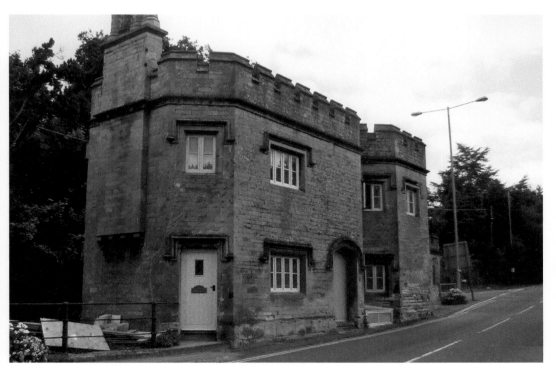

Shane's Castle.

At the foot of the hill, and forming the main access from the town, the asymmetrical Gateway was the last part of the castle curtilage to be built, in around 1860. Picturesque like the castle itself, castellations and arrowslits abound, and it rejoices in a fine arched door. On the large round tower and lower square tower which flank the gateway there are crenellated, machicollated parapets on top of the towers and above the linking arch, on the face of which is a coat of arms. To the town front there are only slit windows but facing the castle, the round tower has small deeply recessed Norman windows and three larger ones with leaded casements.

Toll houses, which usually lie low and consist of very few rooms, are a defunct feature of highways. In Devizes things are different, for at the very sharp junction where the road to Trowbridge meets the Chippenham Road stands Shane's Castle (OS Ref: ST 997617). It is diminutive compared to

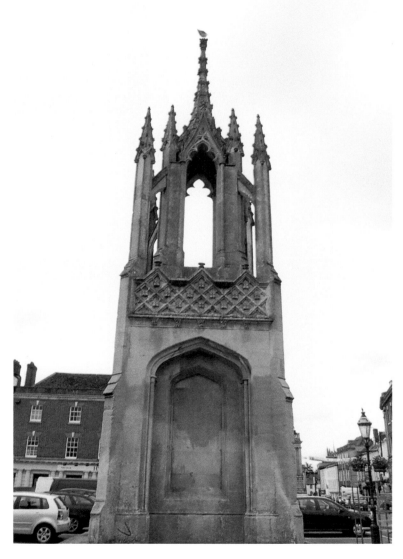

The Market Cross at Devizes.

Devizes Castle, but is considerably more palatial than most toll houses due to being extended. A two-storey stone building, it was constructed in the form of an octagon joined to a rectangle of the same width with splayed angles, and with a small square one-storey porch at its east end. Its claim to be castle-like rests mainly on its crenellations and the stair turret with its slit windows on the north side, for there is the potential to stand on the flat roof and lord it over the passing traffic.

It is currently lived in by a family, who endure the worst effects of the road, with the building gathering dust and being severely polluted. How it acquired its name is lost in time, though one theory suggests that it was named as such due to the fact that it was built around 1840 or 1850 by a former member of staff at Shane's Castle in Ireland. Or 'shane' could be a corruption of 'sham', which it clearly is.

In the centre of the town is the Market Cross (OS Ref: SU 004615). 30 feet high and looking like a detached piece of ecclesiastical architecture, it is all pinnacles, flying buttresses and lozenge-shaped tracery. Designed by Benjamin Dean Wyatt and L. J. Abington in 1814, it provides a natural focal point for a square bounded by tastefully preserved old houses, but the inscriptions on the sides of the monument have a less pleasant tale to tell. Erected in 'grateful attachment' to Devizes by Henry, Viscount Sidmouth, who rejoiced in his thirty years as the town's recorder (as well as its MP, for he was elected six times), the burghers also used the long-lasting qualities of the monument to publish a warning written in capitals about dishonesty to the citizens of Devizes:

THE MAYOR AND CORPORATION OF DEVIZES AVAIL THEMSELVES OF THE STABILITY OF THIS BUILDING TO TRANSMIT TO FUTURE TIME THE RECORD OF AN AWFUL EVENT WHICH OCCURRED IN THIS MARKET PLACE, IN THE YEAR 1753, HOPING THAT SUCH RECORD MAY SERVE AS A SALUTARY WARNING AGAINST THE DANGER OF IMPIOUSLY INVOKING DIVINE VENGEANCE TO CONCEAL THE DEVICES OF FALSEHOOD AND FRAUD.

ON THURSDAY THE 25TH OF JANUARY 1753, RUTH PIERCE OF POTTERN IN THIS COUNTY AGREED WITH THREE OTHER WOMEN TO BUY A SACK OF WHEAT IN THE MARKET, EACH PAYING HER DUE PROPORTION TOWARDS THE SAME. ONE OF THESE WOMEN IN COLLECTING THE SEVERAL QUOTAS OF MONEY DISCOVERED A DEFICIENCY, AND DEMANDED OF RUTH PIERCE THE SUM WHICH WAS WANTING TO MAKE GOOD THE AMOUNT: RUTH PIERCE PROTESTED THAT SHE HAD PAID HER SHARE AND SAID THAT SHE WISHED SHE MIGHT DROP DOWN DEAD IF SHE HAD NOT. SHE RASHLY REPEATED THIS AWFUL WISH: WHEN TO THE CONSTERNATION AND TERROR OF THE SURROUNDING MULTITUDE, SHE INSTANTLY FELL DOWN AND EXPIRED, HAVING THE MONEY CONCEALED IN HER HAND.

Etchilhampton

OS Ref: SU 030598

South-east of Devizes, a traveller on the A342 might be puzzled to see a lion to the side of the road on an exposed, wind-blown spot. This is no beast escaped from a local zoo but the Lydeway Monument, which has been given various other names over the years – including the Wayside Monument and the Long Monument, the latter due to local benefactor James Long. Some

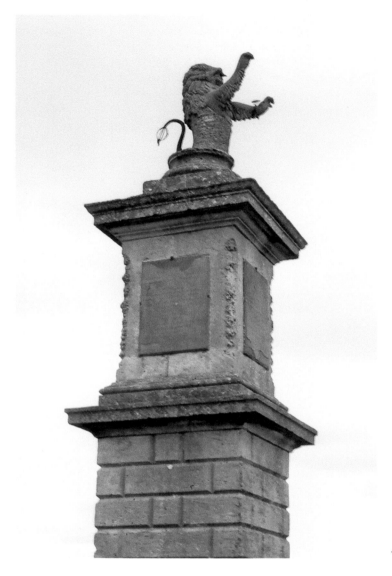

The Lydeway Monument.

5 metres high, it commemorates the building of a road, and it is unknown why the builder chose a lion with its front paws clawing at the air, which is a somewhat unusual pose. There are plaques on all four sides of the plinth which supports the statue. The ones on the east, west and south sides were inscribed with the same words before they ceased to be legible due to weathering, though the plaque on the east side can still be read:

THIS MONUMENT
FROM A GENERAL SENSE OF GRATITUDE
WAS ERECTED TO THE MEMORY OF
JAMES LONG
LATE OF WEDHAMPTON ESQRE

WHOSE PUBLICK SPIRIT AND BENEVOLANCE
WHICH HE EVER EXERCISED FOR THE SERVICE
OF MANKIND, WERE REMARKABLY EXERTED
IN PLANNING, PROMOTING AND COMPLEATING THIS NEW ROAD

AN: DOM. 1768
BY WHICH
A FORMER TEDIOUS AND DANGEROUS WAY
OVER THE ADJACENT HILL
IS AVOIDED
TO GREAT PLEASURE
AND CONVENIENCE OF TRAVELLERS
IN RECTO DECUS

Still just legible on the back is the inscription:

BY PERMISSION
OF MICHAEL TICH.
ESQ

'Tich' was one Tichbourne, who owned the land on which the monument stands. Thus, the road was built over high ground from Devizes to Wedhampton, a village about three 3 to the east, and travellers were spared a ride, which was claimed to be dangerous, over an adjacent hill that overlooks the Vale of Pewsey.

Euridge

OS Ref: ST 833721; Postcode: SN14 8BJ

The achievements of Julian and Isabel Bannerman are world-famous, and their work in Wiltshire is among their finest. Starting his career as a sculptor of relatively small objects in wood, Julian has weaved his magic and expanded his skills to designing whole houses made of stone, while Isabel mainly focusses on the planting, and now shell work, at Euridge Manor. Here they have excelled in their creation of a *jardin clos* with an eclectic ensemble of architectural and horticultural features. Their client is John Robinson, the founder of the very successful Jigsaw label of women's clothing, which has enabled him to build to his heart's desire.

Work started in 1999 and was substantially complete by 2008, and it was clear that John Robinson was planning a significant re-orientation of the estate, not a mere add-on to an old manor house. This was given a large Tudor-style extension which faced south down the valley, making the original house look almost like the extension. On one side he added a Pool House with water bubbling out of a rockery, above which stands an urn. On the walls is some remarkable shell work depicting dolphins and octopuses either side of the staircase. A group of stalactites, some real, some false, stab down from the ceiling. On top of the Pool House a formal garden with topiary has been created, at the end of which there is blind Gothic window forming part of a wall. Next to this stands the long, Italian-style Orangery with a terracotta render. Inside, classical statuary, urns and a large internal rusticated classical façade with columns and a pediment feature.

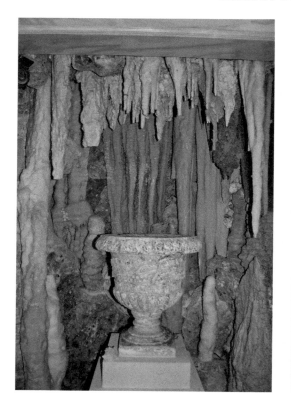

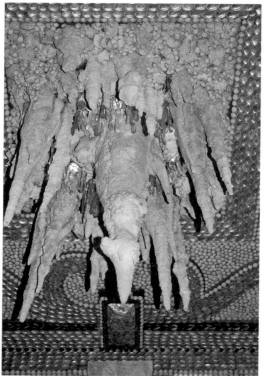

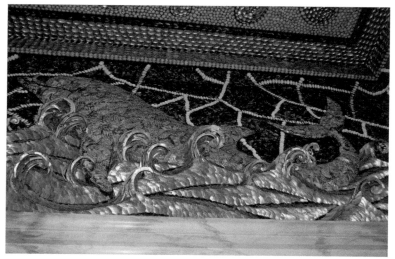

Above left: The bath house urn in the Pool House Grotto at Euridge Manor.

Above right: The Pool House Grotto.

Left: A shell panel at Euridge Manor.

The Bannermans describe what they did as 'architectural shenanigans', insomuch that they created what looks like a medieval monastic settlement, but which is really nothing of the sort; essentially, it is a conceit. The biggest of the mock medieval follies is the Gatehouse, which is made of Bath stone quarried on the estate and is complete with a pointed arch entrance and a small

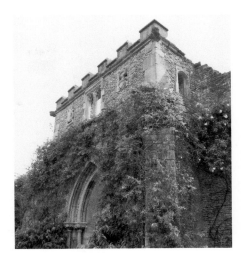

The Gatehouse.

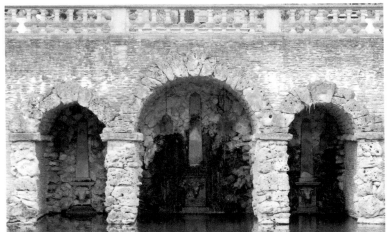

The Grotto façade.

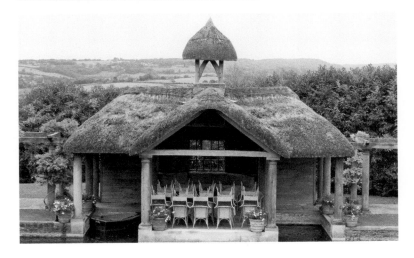

The Boathouse at
Euridge Manor.

window, above which rambling roses climb. A metal spiral staircase leads up to an open floor and one ducks through a low arch to each a small terrace with crenellations. A false ruinous wall extends away from the Gatehouse for some 30 metres, and to add to the conceit, cracks were made in the wall to make it look more authentic.

Below the Tudor extension and its terrace garden lies the remarkable pool, which acts as a tank, collecting water from the house and recycling it for the irrigation of the garden. Facing the pool stands Martin Gane's three-arched Grotto, dating from 2004. Apart from obelisks on the back wall of each chamber, it is relatively undecorated, but decorous in its effect. One can even row a boat into it. Such vessels are normally kept tied up on the other side of the pool at the Boathouse. An open-sided folly, thatched like many of Julian Bannerman's other buildings, it has a circular 'hat' finial and curved benches inside. Set in the water in this part of the pool are matching obelisks and bull's head fountains gushing water from four mouths. Closer to the Grotto on either side of the pool, small wooden duck houses have been placed. These are replicas of the Tudor house. Euridge Manor is an estate transformed into something very special by not just the Bannermans, but a small army of skilled tradesmen and craft workers.

Fonthill

Several around OS Ref: ST 918310

Fonthill is probably the most intriguing of all Wiltshire's private estates for a number of reasons: its creator had a reputation which spread across all levels of society; few people were ever invited there; and the colossal nature of the architectural folly that was built at great expense and at several attempts. Alone, these elements may have been considered less remarkable, but combined they amounted to a heady brew of intrigue, extravagance and obsession thanks to one man – William Beckford. Beckford was a figure of great culture and learning, who tantalised the world with his works of fiction, a series of dissimulations and romantic liaisons considered illicit at the time, as well as a voracious appetite for collecting the finest art works.

The son of the wealthy politician and sugar baron, the so-called Alderman Beckford was typical of a very small minority of Englishmen in the eighteenth century who did not need to go out and work thanks to the wealth that their parents had built up, and therefore could turn their attention to leisure, the arts and, in the case of William Beckford, extravagant building. Embracing the Romantic imagination, Beckford buried himself in literature and art, often exotic and mystical, which provided fuel for his own writings and plans for buildings that were out of scale, highly ornate and stretched his finances. The difference between him and other Romantics was his ability to combine his imagination with his wealth in a series of building projects, which eventually nearly bankrupted him.

Beckford's inspiration for the design of Fonthill Abbey came mainly from buildings in Portugal, where he stayed for several years in his early adulthood following a scandal caused by his homosexual relationship with Kitty Courtney. First, the brilliant white Tower of Belém on the River Tagus shore in Lisbon with its decorative features seemed the perfect example of the meditative tower that had obsessed Beckford since his adolescence. Then, the Monastery of Batalha, with its nave arcade decorated with mouldings and the stained glass windows through which the sun streamed, as well as the octagonal tomb chapel of King João I, gave him Gothic ideas. Then, Beckford rented the finca of Montserrate near Sintra, with its central octagonal plan on a long symmetrical axis, and this also influenced the design of his abbey.

Eventually Beckford came home and work started on the abbey in 1796. Along the way there were various collapses of masonry, notably that of a squat spire in 1800. Eventually he decided to live in the abbey, but to do that he wanted to create more space for his artworks and separate himself from his relatives and hangers-on by extending the building to a very large cruciform. To provide building material, he had no qualms about demolishing Fonthill Splendens, a house still in good condition, but he did not move in until 1807 due to slow progress in the works caused by the lack of craftsman and the unreliability of the architect, James Wyatt. The dimensions of the completed building were extraordinary: a tower 275 feet high; a cruciform plan 350 feet by 290 feet; and long galleries (that of Edward III 68 feet long and Saint Michael 112 feet long). The fan-vaulting supporting the lantern reached 132 feet (40 metres) and the top of the tower was 278 feet (85 metres) from the ground. The quality of the interior was somewhat patchy, for some rooms were small and poorly finished, while other parts were glorious, as Cyrus Redding, the first of Beckford's many biographers, testified about the King Edward Gallery:

> The perfect simplicity which reigned in such an apartment, in which he [Beckford] was careful to introduce nothing that could distract attention; the simple dim shining lamp; the darkly tinted light from the windows, deepening the shadows around the recesses around the Statue [of Edward III], and but the faintly illuminated gilt mouldings; the windows nearly veiled in rich purple, crimson and gold draperies; the organ sending its dep prolonged music along the perspective of the long galleries, while now and then the odour of the incense used in Catholic Worship was used to heighten the effect.

The total cost was never determined, but it is likely to have been many millions of pounds in today's money. The irony is that Beckford only lived there for fifteen years. It was the immense weight on a narrow base and the wood and rubble construction, rather than the foundations or the experimental compo cement, that were partly responsible for the fall of the abbey in a gale in 1825. The parts of the abbey that were built to Wyatt's bad designs and poorly finished by builders were often rectified by stronger rebuilding long before the final collapse.

Lancaster Tower

This sole remainder of Fonthill Abbey is a four-storey, 20-metre crenellated tower that stands in a clearing in front of a wide lawn where the abbey once stood. John Rutter in his 1822 *Description of Fonthill Abbey and Demesne* describes the State Bedroom glowingly in the days of Beckford:

> This handsome room is furnished in a most elegant style: the bed is of crimson silk damask, with very rich fringing...the ceiling is of the purest style of the sixteenth century; round the cornice is richly carved and painted frieze, compose of portcullises and the united roses of York and Lancaster.

Since 2011, Stephen and Bonnie Morant have owned the majority of the old Fonthill estate and have set about a gradual programme of restoration, widening the Western Avenue and cutting down conifers and rhododendrons to clear a view from the Lancaster Tower. The first floor has been beautifully restored, with access by a new cantilevered spiral staircase rising from the ground floor, where a new kitchen and toilets have been built. On either side as you enter the long room there are panelled cupboards, one of these containing a dumb waiter to lift food from the kitchen below.

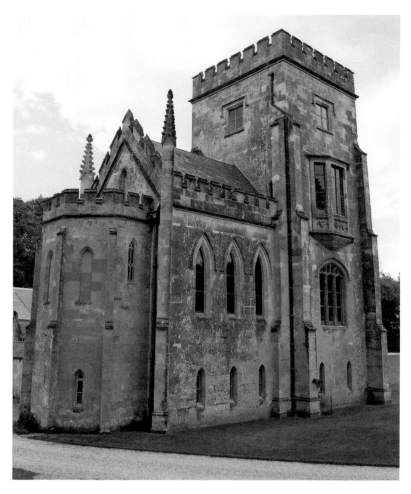

Lancaster Tower.

At the end are two-lighted Gothic windows with stained glass depicting English kings, which were moved from the Brown Dining Room in the abbey. To the left is a gold-framed mirror, and to the right is another window, this time three-lighted. Above, a circular brass candelabra crowns the room. The pinnacle on the connecting range between the tower and new house that the Morants have had built was probably recycled from ruins of the abbey.

Grottoes

There were several grottoes at Fonthill that were once believed to be related to the old house of Fonthill Splendens, and the remains of several can be seen today. The easiest to reach is known as the Cromlech due to its resemblance to a single-chamber megalithic tomb. Situated just above the west bank of Fonthill Lake, it bears a resemblance to the work of the Lanes of Tisbury. Joseph, the elder of the two, was at work for Alderman Beckford around 1761, but Beckford makes no reference to any grottoes in his early writings, and there is very little evidence to identify the builder any of the grottoes on the estate. Whatever the case, it consists primarily of Chilmark limestone, rubble and rough-hewn tufa, jaggedly jutting up and out, but a mushroom of vegetation has overtaken most of it.

On the east of the lake are the lakeside grottoes, which are the remains of the quarry workings once known as the Caves of the Sleepers. Large with several entrances of various sizes, they are barred off to prevent entry. We are led to believe that the grottoes were described by William Beckford in his satirical work *Modern Novel Writing or the Elegant Enthusiast*. In one chapter entitled 'Captivating Scenery' we read of the gardens surrounding Mahogany Castle, seat of Lord Mahogany, and inherited by the hero Charles Oakley (surely a pseudonym for Beckford), who enjoys, relishes and revels in the pleasure of the grotto. The reader is taken down 'irregular steps cut in rock … to the entrance of a spacious cave ... hushed and silent, save that the trickling drops of a purling rill struck in your ear'. And next, 'a broken arch opened to your view the broad clear expanse of the lake, covered with numerous aquatic fowl, and weeping willows adorning the banks'. But Beckford is deceiving us, for Beckford scholar Laurent Châtel tells us that he lifted the description from his half-sister Elizabeth Hervey's novel *Melissa and Mercia*, published in 1788, and it could well be that they were built after this date as no visitors make reference to them until much later.

Then there is the Hermitage. Small and overgrown, but sturdily built with cut stone and mortar, it has masonry concealed behind flints and tufa. But the huts and root houses have all gone, time having taken its toll on these fragile structures. It seems that Josiah Lane was working at Fonthill in 1784, but what he was creating is not clear. The most Beckford would reveal was in a letter to a friend:

> Mr Lane is rockifying, but not on high places, but in a snug copse by the riverside, where I spend many an hour in dreaming [about] my unfortunate princes [Vathec's companions] and contriving reasonable ways and means of sending them to the Devil.

Triumphal Arch and Boathouse

Further north along the west side of the Fonthill Lake stands the most prominent of the smaller buildings, but again it predates William Beckford. Bishop Pococke noted the Triumphal Arch on his travels in 1754, forming a grand taster for Fonthill Splendens. The main house was built by a London builder called Hoare, who may have continued here. He showed a small stylistic debt to Inigo Jones, with its alternate bands of knobby vermiculated rustication, including a huge human face in the keystone of the arch, only recognisable at a short distance. There are two parts to the living accommodation on either side of the road which runs through the building, with urns crowning the pediment and balustrading running along the flat roof. While the Triumphal Arch is of satisfying proportions, the Victorian urns and scrolls which line the approach to it from Fonthill Gifford are gigantic and out of proportion, at some 8 metres high.

Not dissimilar, and possibly also built in the 1750s by Hoare, is the nearby Boathouse. With a plan like a keyhole and vaulted like a crypt with a knobbly central boss, it is now semi-derelict but still serviceable, with the water lapping high against the ambulatory that runs around the edge. The piers are rusticated with frostwork, but the attractive façade once depicted in an early engraving has collapsed, along with the adjoining bays.

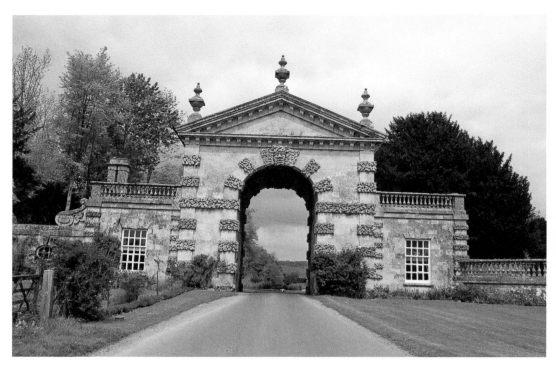

Above: The Triumphal Arch at Fonthill.

Below: The Fonthill Boathouse.

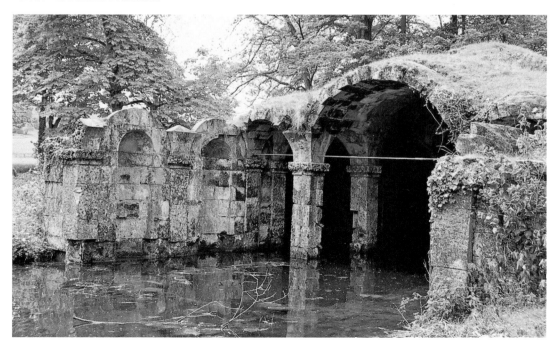

The last word on the estate at Fonthill should come from the Reverend William Lisle Bowles, builder of Maud Heath's Column near Bremhill in the north of Wiltshire:

Enter – from this arch'd portal, look again,
Back, on the lessening woods and distant plain.
Ascend the steps – the high and fretted roof
Is woven by some Elfin hand aloof,
While from the painted windows long array,
A mellow'd light is shed, as not of day.
How gorgeous all! Oh never my spell
Be broken, that array's those radiant forms so well.

Grittleton

Several around OS Ref: ST 857820; Postcode: SN14 6AP

If the London lawyer Joseph Neeld's impact on the village of Grittleton, 6 miles north-west of Chippenham, was considerable, then his folly was even greater. To indulge his fancies he had the good fortune to be left some £660,000 in a will, part of which he invested in the highly prosperous East India Company and in land in London and elsewhere. In 1828 he bought the Grittleton estate from his friend Colonel John Houlton, which he extended and made his principal residence. He became a Member of Parliament but attended the Commons little, one reason being his consuming interest in everything about his newly adopted Wiltshire; now that he had taken root in the county, he hoped to flourish there.

He did indeed flourish, at least in architectural terms, extending Grittleton House into a cavernous house with a Gothic feel, though his accretions have a mishmash of styles. More fanciful are his towers dotted around the estate, which were intended to serve as semaphore posts. Attached to estate cottages, they rise to heights considerably greater than the generally modest and charming dwellings that offered accommodation to Neeld's workers. Situated around the villages of Sevington, Leigh Delamere and Alderton, as well as Grittleton, Neeld created a network of communication points that reflected the trend for semaphores created during the Napoleonic Wars. However, the wars were over, so what was the point of them now? This is hard to determine, and it is harder to imagine that at any time he would have servants signalling from one tower to the next either by waving their arms, reflecting mirrors or lighting beacons.

The most northerly of the lodge towers is Fosse Lodge, which, as its name suggests, is on the Fosse Way. Designed in 1835 by James Thomson as a gamekeeper's lodge, the main house has some nice features, including mullioned windows and drip courses. The tower is hexagonal and about 10 metres tall, finishing in a short parapet with a coat of arms emblazoned on the outside. It is punctuated on each of its six sides with some very small openings alternating with bigger ones containing three ledges for birds to alight on.

There are small towers on the school at Sevington and the stables at West Foscote, but none is as grand as the one that was added to Foscote Lodge, where Neeld's estate agent lived. At least five storeys high, it has some large glazed windows, and its top floor has some well-executed decorative mouldings and an arched window. This tower reaches at least 20 metres, and as the tallest and the nearest, it would be the most likely to have any signals seen from the dumpy, vaguely Italianate

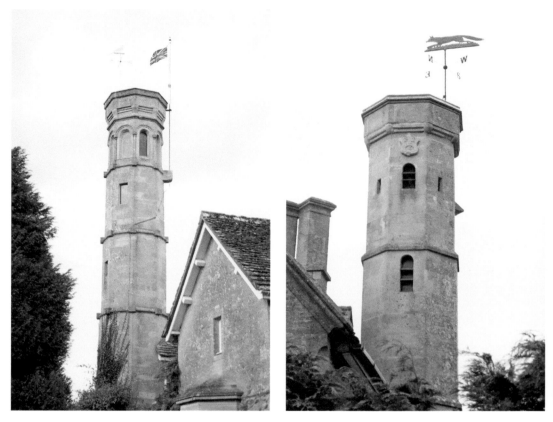

Above left: Foscote Lodge.

Above right: Fosse Lodge.

tower on the main house at Grittleton. Despite its grandiose potential, Neeld's system of signalling collapsed, as did his marriage, due to the discovery of a love child by his newly wed wife. With no legitimate or male heirs, even through his brother, ironically the offspring of the love child eventually inherited the estate.

Iford

OS Ref: ST 801588: Postcode: BA15 2BA

Visiting Iford Manor in May is a glorious riot of wisteria, which engulfs the house and its immediate surroundings, while later in the summer all the focus is on the Cloisters, where operas are staged. Guarded by two Lombardic lions dating from the thirteenth century, this fine building is resplendent with ancient Italian and Byzantine sculpture, masonry, carving and sculpture collected by Sir Harold Peto, the architect who owned the manor in the early twentieth century, and who built this pseudo-religious conceit to express his Roman Catholicism. On the façade and inside are a variety of statues, plaques and other carvings, including a well-head from Aquilegia and a Virgin and Child from Treviso. The building has the look of authenticity with its Romanesque style and wide-eaved roof, round-headed windows and statues of various figures, including a bishop and monk set in niches on the front wall. There are a number of stone plaques and bas reliefs, including two winged putti holding a tree, and rows of marble columns running round the central roofless courtyard. To the south side an opening leads to a balcony – ideal for the dramatic scenes that are played out in the operas.

The upper part of the garden at Iford is remarkable for its Great Terrace – a long promenade bordered by planting and on the south-east side by a colonnade. At the east end is the Gazebo or Tea House, which once stood on a mount in the kitchen garden across the public road, but was moved by Peto. It dates from the eighteenth century and it may have been built by the Gaisford family, who owned the manor then. It affords a fine view over the neighbouring countryside, and is made of limestone ashlar with a slate roof. An elegant octagon with sash windows, its double doors with flanking Ionic pilasters open on to the terrace.

The third building of interest in the garden is the Casita at the far north-west end of the Great Terrace. It consists of a Spanish-style three-bay open loggia, and was built by Harold Peto around 1910, with more examples of his collection, including early thirteenth-century columns from Verona, supporting a carved wooden frieze. The interior of loggia contains several fragments of sculptured carving, including two roundels, one including an Agnus Dei, a semi-circular niche containing a French statue, as well as flanking billet-moulded panels with reliefs from Naples.

The Kitchen Garden at Iford Manor is significantly different in style from the Peto Garden in its planting, for example, of low box hedges, some of which have been turned into animal-shaped topiary. It is here that the creative genius and deep knowledge of myths and legends possessed by Iford Manor's current owner, Elizabeth Cartwright-Hignett, have been displayed in all its glory. This is the garden of regeneration, littered with its symbolism from ancient and more modern times.

At the top of the garden stands the Pavilion of the Green Man, which is an altogether unusual building. Originally built by Cartwright-Hignett's mother in the late 1960s as a place for picnicking and entertaining friends, the pavilion has had its interior transformed by its current owner. Its plain classical exterior does not prepare you for the cornucopia of decoration that seems to flow from the walls. Covered with representations of pagan, classical and wildlife figures made of pieces of ceramic, shells, pebbles and glass, this mosaic covers the entire interior in an all-embracing and narrative way. The figures are not standard representations, but Cartwright-Hignett's own versions of some well-known figures, while others are her creations, bearing no resemblance to anything in folklore or mythology.

However, we are certain that large face that confronts us on the back wall of the pavilion is that of the Green Man, who watches you with his large eyes. He has a tree for a body, out of which grow branches where birds sit, and very large hands in which he holds the beings he has created. Most obvious is the figure of a man-like being holding up his arms in reverence, formed out of the little finger of his left hand. Sitting in his right hand there is another reverential half-human, half-bird creature, with a long brown beak, red feet and head, and a coat of black and white feathers. Recognised since Roman times, the Green Man slipped in between the pagan and Christian worlds as a figure who sprang from the earth. Nature was let into Church life as a kind of facilitator to the ritual, powerful yet neutral, an observer of all that Man believed.

The characters on the right, or south-east wall, are pushing and pulling the sun with a rope. The character pushing is a half-human, half-animal figure, who looks a little like a satyr but without the malevolence; indeed, he is a bringer of light, with leaves growing out of his body. The sun he is pushing is formed by a bull's eye window of the pavilion, with flames made of ceramic leaping out

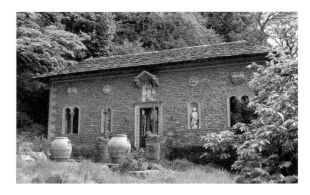

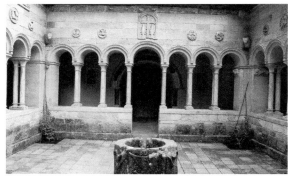

Iford Manor Cloisters.

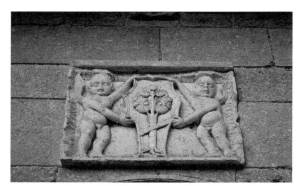

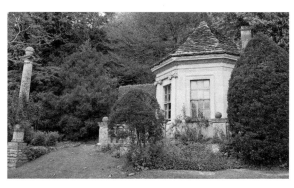

The Iford Manor Gazebo.

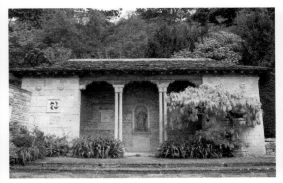 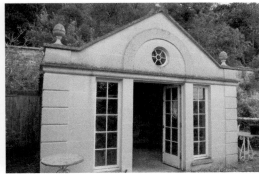

Above left: The Casita.

Above right: The Pavilion of the Green Man.

to the sides. On the right of the sun is a vegetable creature, with a female human body, complete with breasts, and the head of a bird with a sharp beak and a coat of feathers, bringing light to Earth in anticipation of human life. Beneath, a dog-like pet with a humanoid head follows her.

Facing this scene on the left, or north-west wall, another half-human, half-animal kneels on a rock. A little like Anubis, the Egyptian god of death, is this a fox or, more menacingly, a jackal? Its lower half is human, while its eyes look straight at the visitor, staring him out. Again the sun is the bull's eye window, and beyond it is a recumbent four-legged sphinx-like figure with water for hair flowing in blue – a clever use of ceramics. She looks towards the Green Man in admiration, not worship; remember, he is not a god but a slippery character whom no one really dislikes – rather, he is more someone who inveigles his way surreptitiously into your life.

On the front wall there is a rabbit and a hare, and above the door an idiot like Bottom from *A Midsummer Night's Dream* peers over the threshold. To the right, a mainly black bird with tall feathers is perched on a rock. All about the walls of the pavilion are more recognisable animals, particularly rabbits, butterflies and birds, as well as plants – the fruit of the Green Man's magic.

From 1999, the decoration in the Pavilion of the Green Man took two years to plan and collect materials, such was the great care to ensure a quality finish. Collecting takes time, and the provenance of the shells is widespread. Closest to home, many of the mosaics came from a shop on Pulteney Bridge in Bath. The oyster shells which form part of the Green Man came from an oyster bar in Weymouth, discarded in a yard once their insides had been eaten by the diners, and the slipper shells were from the same Dorset coastal town, as well as further east at Sandbanks. Many of the others came appropriately enough from Shell Island, located south of Harlech in North Wales, to where Cartright-Hignett crossed at low tide to scour the beaches, where they say there are 204 varieties. The little shells are from the island of Tiree in the Inner Hebrides, where the Cartwright-Hignetts would holiday.

The enigma continues as one enters the Puzzle Garden through a threshold into which words made of ceramic pieces have been inserted, with one line on each side of the opening:

NOW I WAS HERE WHEN YOU BEGAN
I TRAVEL WITH YOU
CATCH ME IF YOU CAN

And so you reach the puzzle, a most curious chequerboard of pebble squares alternating with low box hedges, each about 50 centimetres square and amounting to an area of about 20 by 10 metres. A design which mixes up the natural with the human-made, there are fifty-four squares, and in the twenty-seven pebble squares are three letters, each being part of a word coming from a four-line poem written by Cartwright-Hignett, scattered in a slightly zigzag fashion across the 'board'. There are some squares with decorative motifs too. Fixed to the upper wall there is a copper plaque covered in a patina of verdigris which shows the pattern, and a little way down the wall is a plaque with the solution to the puzzle:

> TIME IS OUR CHEQUERBOARD OF DARK AND LIGHT
> WITH PEACE AND TURMOIL, GRIEVING AND DELIGHT:
> AND IN THE END THERE'S NO MORE TIME TO TELL
> TO MAKE AMENDS; SO LOVE, AND USE TIME WELL
> ECH

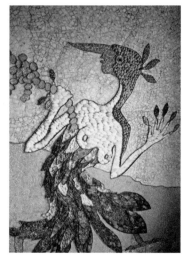

The half-bird, half-woman of Iford Manor.

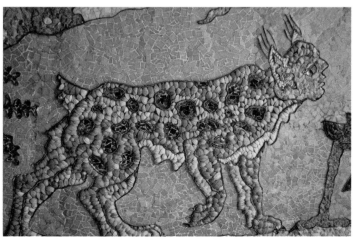

The Iford Manor dog.

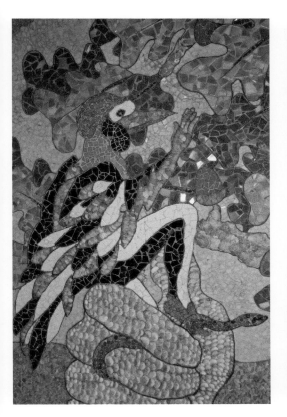

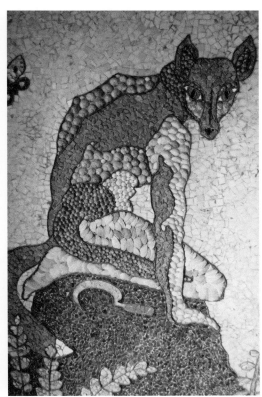

Above left: The Iford Manor bird man.

Above right: Iford Manor fox man.

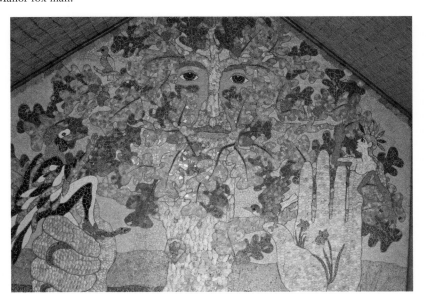

The Green
Man mosaic.

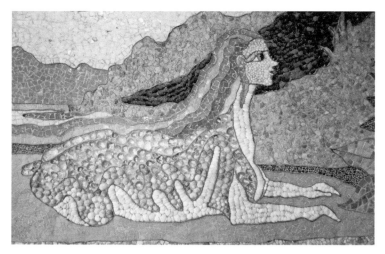

The sphinx of Iford Manor.

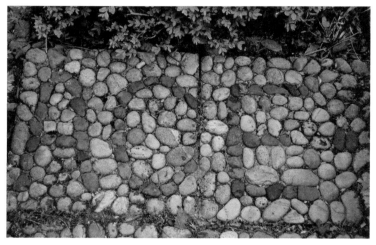

The Puzzle Garden.

Lacock

OS Ref: ST 919684; Postcode: SN15 2LG

Wiltshire has its own sphinx, not next to a pyramid, but on top of the Coupled Columns at Lacock Abbey, the estate once owned by the pioneer of photography William Henry Fox Talbot. On the lawn close to the abbey stands this curious garden feature, but it has not always been here. An 1804 watercolour of Devizes Market Place shows it as a dominant feature, taller than the buildings around the edge of the square. This must be artistic licence, for at Lacock it stands about 20 feet high, and the apparent lion in the watercolour has changed to a sphinx, sitting on two fluted Doric columns on a pedestal decorated with a cartouche on the north side and lozenges on each end. Benjamin Carter has been attributed as the sculptor of the sphinx, but this is unlikely as he died much before 1804, when the columns were in Devizes – and in any case they were topped by a lion. The details of its removal to Lacock remain unknown.

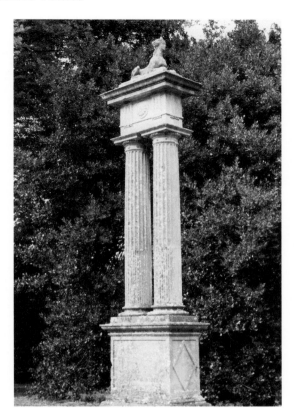

Coupled Columns with a sphinx.

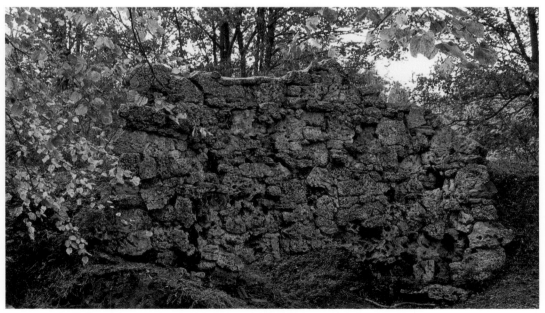

The Lacock Grotto.

There is a plain Gothic Alcove in the rose garden to the north of the abbey, but this is not as intriguing as the other main curiosity – the Grotto. Standing at the far end of the grounds on the other side of a stream, it is more an elaborate rockwork with numerous boulders, mainly tufa, piled to create a very block or knobbly and irregular masonry, but it has no interior for sitting in melancholy or running water to cool oneself on a hot day. The sculpture of a reclining bull has been placed on top, making this edifice all the more curious. It seems that the Grotto formed part of a formal garden in the North Park and was simply an ornament that completed the view. It is not proven that Capability Brown had anything to do with it, although he worked here briefly in 1755 and 1765, being paid £250 for his work – apparently his efforts were quite modest and hard to discern compared to some of his more dramatic changes.

Ludgershall

OS Ref: SU 295510; Postcode: SP11 9DN

After Biddesden House was bought in 1931 by Bryan Walter Guinness, later Lord Moyne, the garden took on its present character. Once he employed George Kennedy, the garden became primarily ornamental rather than a working farm or kitchen garden. Kennedy may have been responsible for the first garden building of interest that the visitor encounters, as it stands just to the north-east of the house, an early twentieth-century wooden Temple with deep portico. The tympanum depicts a harlequin playing the flute as well as a cat and various birds, mainly doves, fluttering and splashing around. Now in a poor state, it could take pride of place at the top end of the lawn if it were in better condition. Another Temple is buried in an overgrown orchard. Made mainly of pale stone, it incorporates an early nineteenth-century wooden portico that formerly adorned the south front of the mainly red brick house.

The true gem of this estate is a little way out of sight of the house, situated at the north-west corner of the walled garden. The Gazebo, or Pool House, dating from 1933, is made of flint and brick, and has an irregular shape, around which the moat-like pool curves. Above is a pediment crowning a square wing, while a circular copper dome is finished with a large ball finial. The trick

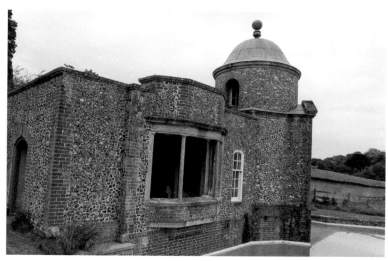

The Pool House at Biddesden House.

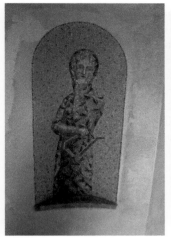
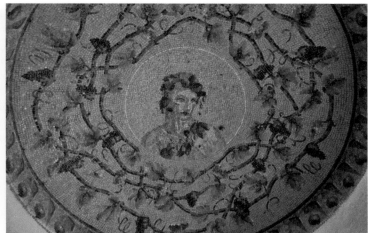

Above left: The mosaic of Erato at Biddesden House.

Above right: The mosaic of Apollo at Biddesden House.

here is to jump through the unglazed oriel window into the pool, enjoy the rest of the day in the warm sun, and forget the superb decoration inside the gazebo. It is likely that any swimmer will have passed through the changing rooms, whose most outstanding feature is a series of mosaics dating from 1937 by Boris Anrep, a Russian sculptor active in Britain in the early to mid-twentieth century. Slightly art deco in style, the mosaics depict three muses – Erato, Clio and Thalia – who are set in niches that surround a domed ceiling with a mosaic of Apollo as a hunter. Exotic, colourful pheasants and plants decorate the floor.

The wall of the main chamber has a painting by Roland Pym of a nymph astride a seahorse, surrounded by shells, and above is a fierce classical god with festoons. A naked Venus by Italian sculpture Ernesto Gazzeri, sculpted in marble, is set in a niche. Kennedy wanted to build four gazebos, one in each corner of the walled garden, but Bryan Guinness baulked at it, perhaps fearful of the costs, given the expense no doubt already lavished on this delightful and unusual bath house.

Marlborough
OS Ref: SU 183686; Postcode: SN8 1PA

The Grotto at Marlborough College is a jewel of decoration, and is one of Wiltshire's finest. Originally created by Frances, Countess of Hertford, she was responsible for some of the landscaping and embellishment of the grounds of the Mansion, as the main house was known in the eighteenth century. She started working on the grotto in about 1735, an early year for this sort of garden feature, creating a building with three connecting chambers standing close to the foot of the Mound – a small hill that was once surmounted by the keep of Marlborough Castle. It is an accomplished creation of thousands of shells, stones and rocks arranged in three connecting chambers, the central one facing the door having a kind of altar with an arch of shells and an urn in the middle bearing the inscription:

AEQUAM MEMENTO
REBUS IN ARDUIS
SERVARE MENTEM

These lines are from the often quotable Roman poet Horace, an example of the eighteenth-century passion for all things classical. The translation, 'remember to keep a clear head in difficult times', may be an indication of the Herculean task the building of the grotto must have been for Lady Hertford – or perhaps she was commenting on national events going on around her.

The approach to the grotto is up tufa-lined steps and past three basins of water often full of water. The top step contains an oval inscription, which declares the grotto was made by Lady Hertford and repaired *c.* 1988 in memory of Harold Cresswell Brentnall (1903–55) a history master of Marlborough College. Inside the grotto there are plaques inscribed 'Your Memory Brentnall shares a lasting place' as well as 'Where Thomson sang of spring and Hertford's grace'. The later are lines by the poet Stephen Duck and refer to James Thomson, who was invited to take part on poetry readings at Marlborough, and who wrote the words for 'Rule Britannia'.

Duck, who was first a Wiltshire labourer who turned priest, and who was then Yeoman of the Guard, responsible for Queen Caroline's grotto at Richmond, would later become Frances' favourite. At Marlborough, his praise for her is preserved on a stone plaque:

> Within the basis of a verdant Hill;
> a beauteous Grot confesses Hertford's skill;
> Who, with her lovely Nymphs, adorns the Place;
> Gives ev'ry polished Stone its proper grace;
> Now varies rustic moss about the Cell;
> Now fits the shining Pearl or purple Shell …

From above, water drips down in a series of shells, one beneath the other, and eventually into a pool at the back of the central chamber, past gleaming crystals, conches, shells, tufa and horses' teeth. The grotto has a brick shell upon which the decorations have been encrusted and a red brick and tile floor, while the ceiling is studded with jagged rocks. The two side chambers each have three niches in their design, with a small light hole at the top of the two niches which face outwards. These are encrusted with darker shells nearer the top, perhaps to give the effect of the night sky.

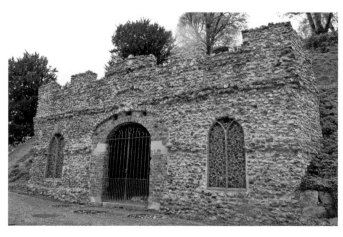

The shell grotto at Marlborough.
(G. and M. Hull)

Such fine work had fallen into disrepair by the 1980s, when Diana Reynell (1933–2017), who was teaching jewellery at Marlborough College, took the initiative to restore the grotto. She enlisted the help of her pupils, requiring them to saw up horses' teeth. To get a flavour of what a particular task it is to authentically restore such a special decorative curiosity, she describes the difficulty of finding exactly the right quality of blue 'glass' slag for the Marlborough grotto:

> All that time I was keeping an eye out, asking everyone I met. Many blind alleys e.g. glass "frit", "end of day" glass at Stourbridge, searching from place names for C18 factories – "Glasshouse hill", glassmakers at Salisbury, in Surrey, in Bristol. Finally after 4 years of this, one of these conversations and the production of a sample led straight to a certain field, on a Herefordshire farm, a range of stone buildings which had been an Ironworks, 1720 cut into the wall, and the perfect match of blue "glass" trodden in a gateway, scattered in a field, and finding its way over the centuries into a nearby stream. It is C18 furnace slag, the particular blue coming from the chemical mix in the furnace at that time (copper used).

Reynell had known the Marlborough grotto for '20 years of sordid neglect before there was any money to work with. It was good luck at the end of that time to find Simon Verity living close by, who was obviously raring to go on grottoes, and have the skilful lettering and carving from his workshop to replace so imaginatively the lost centre of the grotto'.

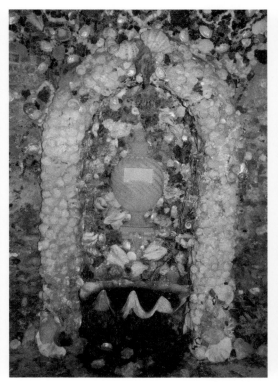 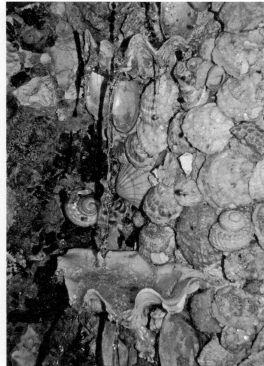

Above left: The shell house's decorated wall panel. (G. and M. Hull)

Above right: The shell house's water feature. (G. and M. Hull)

Melksham

OS Ref: ST 897897; Postcode: SN12 8DG

Along a narrow alleyway between fences behind a house on Bath Road in Melksham lies the Outdoor Studio. It is a creation of the 1990s recession in the building trade, when architect Alvin Howard had little to do but build a folly garden with a series of nine national and other themes – French, Mediterranean, Chinese and American among them – all squeezed in a quarter of an acre. His wife Judith designed the interior touches, with the result being a confection of different styles in a space little more than 30 metres long and less than 10 metres wide.

One of the first buildings to catch your eye is the Chinese Pavilion, based on the one at Shugborough, Staffordshire. Approached over a small bridge, one enters the empire of the senses. Partly sheltered by a sumach tree, it is painted with grey and red lacquer, with a gold finial to finish the roof. Little lanterns hang down and the bamboo blinds keep prying eyes from seeing any who dare rest among the blue and white porcelain. Facing the pavilion is the Summer House; once a tea house on the Kennet & Avon Canal, when rescued from decay it had to be reassembled. With a frilly white fascia board and some pretty Gothic windows, it is painted an attractive pale blue and serves as Judith's studio.

The Howards converted and added a steeple and a finial in the shape of a cat to an old asbestos shed they found in the plot of land that came with the house. They turned this into a brilliant white clapboard Mock American Church, with electricity and running water to make tea for afternoon parties. At the end of the garden the Grotto is a simple open affair, made with shells – mainly scallops – collected from local fishmongers. They are fixed to a stone wall that is dominated by the face of a river god, which drips water in to a pool. This is the Howards' homage to Stourhead. Their white wooden dovecote is a copy of the Gothick Temple at Bramham Park in Yorkshire, while the Treehouse was inspired by one of the earliest at Pitchford Hall in Shropshire. Beautifully finished with lozenge-shaped cuts in the balustrade that mimic the leaded lozenge windows, and an elegant carved fascia board, it has soft furnishings inside, making it a delightful retreat.

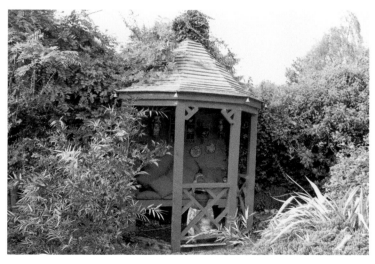

The Chinese pavilion at Melksham, at the Outdoor Studio.

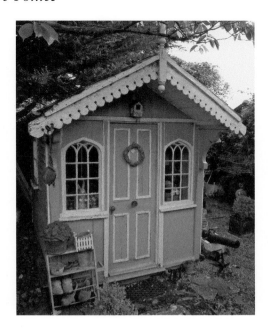

The Summer House, now the Outdoor Studio.

This is a garden that runs with water, with pools, channels and dripping fountains. It is a peaceful haven. Alvin Howard sums up his philosophy: 'It's an architectural design-led garden. We aren't plant people and it's meant to be fun. Folly gardens tend to be created during recessions, as ours was. It's a form of distraction, and helps to take your mind off difficult times.'

Middle Woodford

OS Ref: SU 128364; Postcode: SP4 6NT

The junction of two channels running off the Hampshire Avon near the village of Middle Woodford offers the opportunity for some kind of architectural playfulness. The answer is a Japanese Teahouse, accurate to the last detail standing over the confluence in the grounds of Heale House, which dates from the late sixteenth century. With its fine red brick contrasting with the green of a lovely garden next to a plant nursery, this is a beautiful spot north of Salisbury. Heale House was one of several hiding places for King Charles II after the many skirmishes he had to escape from, this time in 1651. The estate was originally owned by the Hyde family, but was eventually bought in 1894 by Louis Greville, a diplomat who restored and enlarged it between 1898 and 1910, with advice from the architect Detmar Blow (1867–1939). From 1906 to 1911, Greville created, with the assistance of Harold Ainsworth Peto, a series of formal gardens, including a Japanese garden influenced by Greville's experiences while he was working at the British Embassy in Tokyo. On his return to England in 1900 he transported a number of ornaments, including a huge stone temple lantern and several smaller snow lanterns.

Greville also brought over four Japanese garden experts who built the teahouse, complete with a thatched roof and circular windows with rice paper shutters, which, when open, reveal impressive views over the valley. It has eight *tatami*, or floor mats, in the waiting bay and an equal

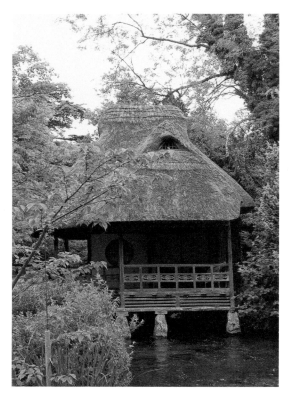

Left: The Tea House at Heale House.

Below: The balcony of the Tea House.

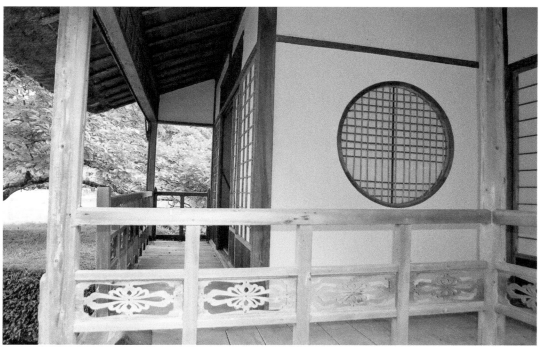

number in the tea room. The intrigue of the Orient is heightened by the sliding partitions and openings, which reveal a raised stove in a corner when opened. Pink and white are the dominant colours and a terrace takes you round the house. Close by is a traditional Nikko Bridge, based on one in Japan, and the scene is complemented by magnificent magnolia and walnut trees.

The teahouse stands over a small brick-lined channel, which forms part of the late seventeenth-century water-meadow irrigation system. The layout of the whole garden has since been simplified and replanted, while the Japanese garden now displays water-loving plants, mainly introduced in the late twentieth century. The supporting stanchions of the teahouse were sited in the water so as to make the river ripple in an appealing way. Inside it is tastefully furnished in the traditional nineteenth-century Japanese style. Altogether, it is a very pleasant place to relax.

Monkton Farleigh

OS Ref: ST 755661

Browne's Folly is often known locally as the Pepperpot for its slight resemblance to a condiment container, but it is more in the style of Bath, being faintly like those hill-top towers of Tuscany that have been copied in the city. Its position overlooking the Avon Valley was exploited in the Second World War for observation and surveying purposes when a tent was placed on top by the Ordnance Survey, and one can still see the Bristol Channel and the Westbury White Horse on a clear day. Lacking in decoration and with blind windows which give an unwelcoming look,

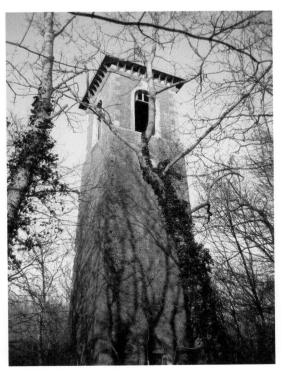

Browne's Folly.

perhaps its upper floor deserves most attention, with its deep eaves, round-arched openings and balustraded handrails, though parts of these are missing. The inscription on a tablet 20 feet up says:

W 1848 B

E

C 1907 H

'WB' was Wade Browne, a quarry owner who had purchased the manor estate in Monkton Farleigh in 1842, and in 1848 he had the tower erected, as the 'E' suggests. 'CH' was Charles Hobhouse, a subsequent owner of the estate, who inserted the tablet in 1907 and used the tower for luncheon rendezvous for his shooting parties.

Wade Browne was a significant benefactor of a variety of causes, and it is said that he built the tower to relieve unemployment in Bathford, situated in the valley below. He also improved the road at Farley Wick Green, had water piped from Ash Well to the communal pump in Monkton Farleigh and donated a barrel organ for the church. His interest in local education went as far as founding a school, where he personally taught the girls.

In the late twentieth century, the Wildlife Trust acquired the land but did not wish to be responsible for the tower as it was a building and therefore outside the normal remit of their conservation activities. So they gifted it to the Folly Fellowship, which did not have the funds to restore it in full, but provided an interim solution for the stabilisation of the structure by installing a new, shallow, pyramidal copper roof.

Newton Toney

OS Ref. SU 222414; Postcode: SP4 0HS

In 1709, the architect William Benson, the High Sheriff of Wiltshire, took possession of the Wilbury estate, and later he replaced Sir Christopher Wren as Surveyor of the Works at Saint Paul's Cathedral, making more money out of his brief stay in office than Wren had in the previous forty years. With the earnings he built Wilbury House in the Inigo Jones revival style in order to give himself the appropriate standing for a political career, as well as a few follies for his pleasure.

The features in the grounds include two undecorated grottoes. In Grotto Wood, around 200 metres to the south-west of the house, is Benson's Grotto, an early eighteenth-century flint grotto. With a short entrance passage that curves round inside a bank, it consists of a square chamber set into the earthen bank. Barbara Jones claims that it is a very early example of Gothic, probably based on the atmosphere evoked by its style: it has a symmetrical square vaulted chamber 4 metres high, the crossing of the vault is emphasised with thin slabs of stone set edgewise and plain red brick arches throw deep shadows into curved niches opposite the entrance and to both sides, offsetting the flint very well. It contains two rustic seats made of gnarled branches placed in the large niches.

The other grotto stands about 200 metres to the north-east of the house and lies under the Summerhouse Grotto, an early eighteenth-century building reaching a height of nearly 10 metres, and which has been restored most recently in the early twenty-first century. This grotto has a domed vault of flint and stone, but its purpose seems purely decorative and it is unlikely to

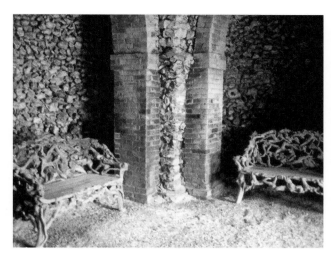

Grotto seats in Benson's Grotto at
Wilbury House.

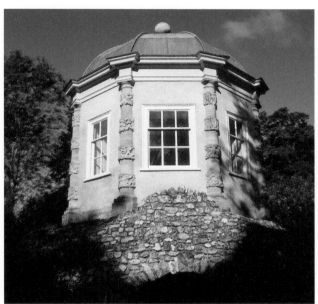

The Summerhouse Grotto at
Wilbury House.

have been either an ice house or a boathouse as has been suggested as the lie of the land does
not lend itself to the creation of a lake. The summerhouse above is octagonal with a zinc domed
roof and is approached by ten steps with a balustrade. It has Tuscan half-columns with banded
rustication and a pretty umbrella porch, with hollow shells and lions' heads as finials to the ribs
of the umbrella. Inside, it has a domed ceiling made of matchboard. Dating from the early to
mid-eighteenth century, it may have been built in Benson or Hoare's time.

The final feature of interest on the estate came much later – a monument commemorating
Queen Victoria's Diamond Jubilee in 1897. Made of limestone, it is a short Ionic column with
a large capital supporting a large handled urn, fluted around the cup, and vine leaf and mask
decoration around the sides.

Oare

OS Ref: SU 156630; Postcode: SN8 4JH

Although Sir Clough Williams-Ellis designed two new wings as well as various outbuildings at Oare House, the creator of Portmeirion, the greatest folly park in Wales, did not design anything follyish apart from a small Palladian loggia. However, another famous architect, Ieoh Ming Peh, did step in to complete the scene with the Millennium Pavilion, a strikingly modern twist on a well-tried folly type – the eyecatcher. Best known for the pyramid at the Louvre in Paris, I. M. Peh finished the lime avenue from the house with another glass pyramid. Concrete on the ground floor, and with projecting beams supported by steel rods providing stability, it may have less of the Chinese American's obsession for just the right type of material that the Louvre has, but the care is still there. Here the panes are large and square, framed in steel, and reaching a height of 15 metres. Above the service rooms on the ground floor it has essentially just one room – a hexagonal lounge that rises to a square and then a pointed roof with a ball finial. Here all can be seen in a transparent structure; this is a radical shift from the privileged, hidden world where the owners used to sit in isolation from their servants.

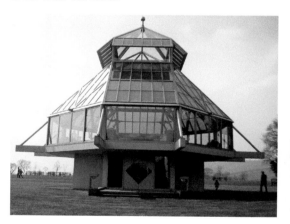
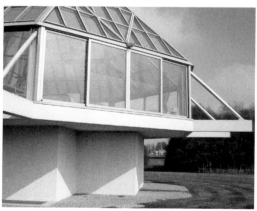

The Millennium Pavilion.

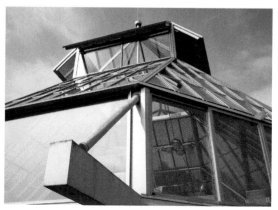

The pavilion's commissioner was Mrs Henry Keswick. Clearly a bold client, she defied the conventions of what a garden building is supposed to be – classical, Gothic, baroque or whatever. This is shock of the new, a totally unexpected building in a part of Wiltshire that expects convention, but it is not totally rootless in its updating of the architecture of the land of Mr Peh's ancestors.

Salisbury

OS Ref: SU 147303; Postcode: SP1 3UZ

Bourne Hill House, once Wyndham House, is a fine building that has been council offices for many years, and gave its name to the neighbouring public Wyndham Park, which once formed part of the house's garden. Up the rise stands Bourne Hill Porch, looking like an extravagant ornament, but unusually, it has ecclesiastical roots. Dating from the fifteenth century, it was originally Saint Thomas's Porch, part of the north transept of Salisbury Cathedral. In 1791 James Wyatt, an architect who worked more flamboyantly in the county, notably at Fonthill, was carrying out restorations and the porch was found to be too small, so he placed it close to Wyndham House. His client was Henry Penruddock Wyndham, who wanted his gardens embellishing. While it may well have been visible from the house 200 years ago, it certainly is not today, as the view has been obscured by trees and it stands to the east far from the house, near the top of the hill.

Engravings of the cathedral shown that the porch was originally flat-roofed, but Wyatt added an octagonal spire and pinnacles, and a shallow elliptical vault with false ribs, while preserving the rich fifteenth-century leaf carving in the form rosettes on the inside of the arches. The sale particulars of Wyndham House of 1871 describe it as 'an interesting archaeological object, and a charming feature of this valuable property'. It is an unusual place to shelter, but there are no seats to sit down to admire the view of the park.

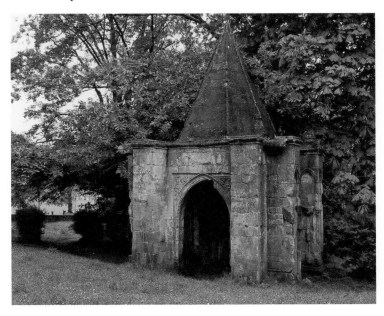

The Bourne Hill Porch.

Seend

OS Ref: ST 942609; Postcode SN12 6NX

Ornamentation and flowering run riot at Seend Manor, an eighteenth-century house surrounded by an extensive estate, whose finest contents are to be found in the 1.5-acre walled garden. Since 1997 Stephen and Amanda Clark have owned the property, dividing their lives between Wiltshire and Hong Kong, where they run businesses, and they have poured their resources into creating one of the most varied gardens in Wiltshire. They have been well served by the ingenious Julian and Isabel Bannerman, who have created something special in transforming the garden into four national themes: England, Italy, Africa and China – countries which reflect their tastes and connections.

The garden is split into four quadrants separated by hornbeams planted in gravel and with a fountain, or *spugna*, of moss-encrusted tufa forming the axis. These allées help transition the visitor between a lime-washed Italian loggia, a miniature thatched cottage, Egyptian sphinxes and then a Chinese pavilion through hedges. First, 'England' is festooned in roses in summer, many of them climbing over the central Gazebo, while in the corner is a Cottage Orné, very much in the Bannerman style, with pinnacles jutting out of a thatched roof, four green oak pillars and an icicle frieze running around the front. 'Africa' reminds Stephen Clark of where he grew up. It contains a simple African Hut coloured pink and red on its walls and with a straw roof tapering to a point. There are obelisks and a sphinxes supplied from stone ornament company Haddonstone. The vegetation is equatorial too, with bananas, reeds and Chusan palm trees. Beyond, there is the Grotto Corner, with a Tufa Arch to pass through to reach the Grotto itself. A wall here is made of some fine minerals and stones, some of which are made of reconstituted pebbles, all dripping towards the pool beneath.

In 'China' the Bannermans played no part because the Clarks were knowledgeable enough of Chinese culture to have a very good idea of what they wanted. The centrepiece is the *ting*, or Pavilion of Past Joys and Present Happiness. The Clarks formed their ideas from the gardens in Suzhou, and consulted many books, before finally drawing one up to their own design. A master craftsman from Hangzhou supervised the construction in Zhuhai, and had it separated into pieces for reassembly in Seend – a task which took eighteen months. It is full of classical allusions such as the twelve antique hitching posts each topped with a *foo* dog, the mythical lion-dog that guards against evil spirits. In the surrounding garden there are more stone dogs, plants such as bamboo and tree peonies, yin and yang shapes, patterns of pebbles and a Chinese studded door.

The final quadrant is 'Italy', beloved by the Clarks for its art and architecture. Here the focus is on entertainment and leisure, with a swimming pool and a Loggia at either end. A stone trough is filled with ice from time to time to keep the wine chilled. Still in the Italian style, there stands against a wall a magnificent Neptune Fountain, inspired by Bernini's Fountain of the Four Rivers in Rome, and adorned with water spouts designed by Stephen Clark.

Outside the walled garden, one can perambulate off-track to the Gazebo, a simple two-storey red brick outhouse. Overlooking the countryside to the south is the Mock Gothic Ruin, with pointed tracery and broken sloping walls. There is even a section with a deliberate constructional 'joke', where a gap in the bricks has been made.

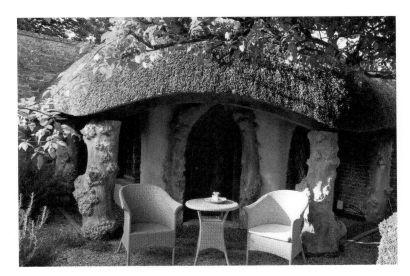

The Cottage Orné at
Seend Manor.

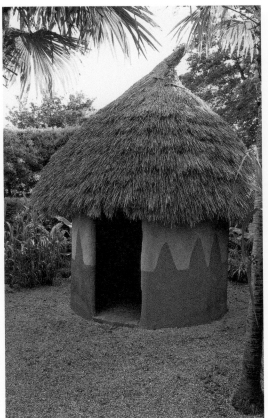

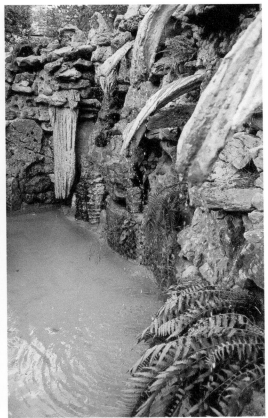

Above left: The African Hut at Seend Manor.

Above right: The Grotto.

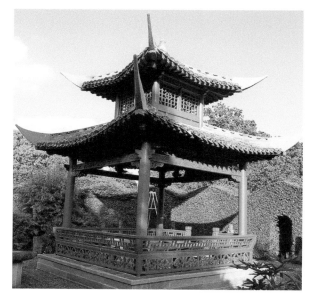

The Pavilion of Past Joys and
Present Happiness.

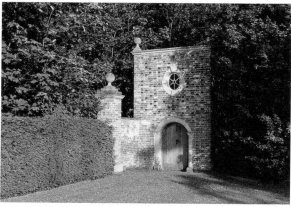

The Gazebo.

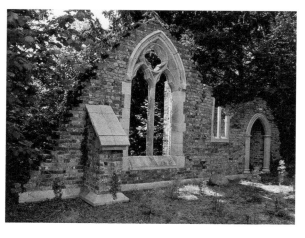

The Mock Ruin.

Stourhead

Several around OS Ref: ST 780340; Postcode: BA12 6QD

Stourhead is one of those landscapes that stays in the mind like a favourite painting. The public's interest in its development has been immense since it first opened its gates, but there is also much folly interest outside the landscape garden's boundaries.

Its creator was Henry Hoare II, the so-called 'Magnificent' (1705–85), an inspired amateur with no previous training or experience of landscape design, gardening or architecture. Derived from a passion enkindled by what he saw on the Grand Tour in Italy and the paintings of the masters of the picturesque Claude Le Lorrain and Nicolas Poussin, he rejected the plans of others, so the landscape is all his conception. An inscription on his memorial in Saint Peter's Church says:

> Here with pure love of smiling Nature warm'd
> This far-fam'd Demy-Paradise he form'd
> And happier still, here learn'd from Heaven to find
> A Sweeter Eden in a Bounteous mind.

There are several, very different aspects to Stourhead, which is less unified and homogenous than say, Stowe, even though that estate has considerably more follies. The styles of architecture at Stourhead are also varied, with Greco-Roman, Palladian, Gothic, Rustic, Monumental and, at one time, Turkish. All together they are a potpourri of buildings, scattered over several square miles of rolling countryside close to the Somerset border.

Hoare's foresight was to dam the source of the River Stour so that it forms an irregular, roughly triangular lake, around which he conjured a scene out of antiquity, with many references to Virgil's *Aeneid*, but also some very English trimmings. From the initial mammoth tasks of earth-moving and lake creation, the estate evolved slowly over thirty years from 1730 until the point that it can be considered the most divine realisation of *genius loci*. The result is a landscape garden close to a vision of nature perfected that has the appearance of being natural, but in fact it has been very carefully designed by man, evidenced in the planting and the situation of the follies. Barbara Jones described it as: 'Achieving a balance between intimacy and space so just that one wonders if serenity may have a mathematical constant.'

The Bristol High Cross (1765)

The visitor is most likely to be led by its present owners the National Trust to the circuit around the lake, where one follows an anticlockwise circuit punctuated by architectural delights. The trick employed is apparently simple: when one arrives at one folly, one's eye is drawn to the next one across leafy glades. This terrestrial Elysium starts with the Bristol High Cross, a spire-like building about 12 metres high, which sits on a small mound overlooking the lake. It consists of several sections from various dates, the oldest going back to the fourteenth century, with several later additions. Originally standing at the junction of Broad Street and High Street in Bristol, it commemorates the event in 1373 wherein Bristol separated from Gloucestershire and Somerset and became a county in its own right. Then it was moved to College Green, and finally a corner

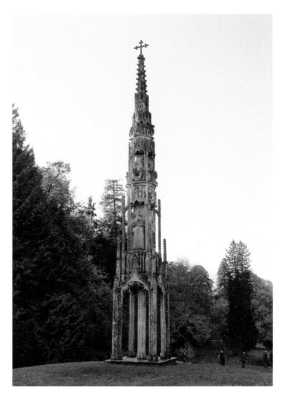

The Bristol High Cross.

of Bristol Cathedral, where it was saved from rotting away thanks to a canon whose brother was the Rector of Stourton. Thus Henry Hoare came to know of it, had it transported to Stourhead in 1764, and re-erected it the following year.

Of an elaborate design in the Decorated Gothic style, the monument contains a series of statues of monarchs, some of whom granted charters to Bristol, and has undergone various restorations and remodellings, the most recent in 1981. Originally painted red, green and gold, the lower tier represents King John, Henry III, and Edward I. It has been suggested that the fourth, being contemporary in style with the others, also represents Edward I, rather than Edward IV as inscribed. The upper storey of kings and queens has Henry VI, Elizabeth I, James I and Charles I, the last suffering the ignominy of temporary removal under the Commonwealth.

Temple Of Flora (1746)

Starting the lake circuit, the first folly encountered is in the Classical theme – the Temple of Flora. Formerly called the Temple of Ceres, the architect of this Tuscan Doric temple was Henry Flitcroft (1697–1769), who was to collaborate with Henry Hoare over many years in integrating the hard architectural elements into the grand design. He was an essentially Palladian architect who rose from humble beginnings to become Comptroller of the King's Works, and designed Wentworth Woodhouse, Wimpole Hall and Woburn Abbey, or at least part of these prodigious piles. The Temple of Flora was built in 1745 with local Chilmark stone, a fine-grained limestone which

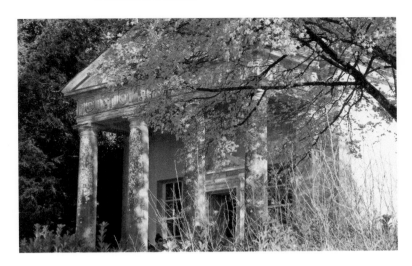

The Temple of Flora.

has for some time shown signs of various lichens growing on it. The building drips with classical allusions, and consists of one room with a portico of four detached columns in the Doric order, and above is a frieze featuring the classical motif of *bucrania*, or goats' skulls.

Ceres, or the Greek goddess Demeter, presided over the Eleusinian Mysteries, into which only initiates were allowed to enter – hence the inscription 'Procul, o procul este profani [Begone, you who are uninitiated! Begone!]' on the temple. These words were used by the Cumaean Sybil to Aeneas as he was about to descent into the underworld, where the story of the founding of Rome was to be revealed to him. It is the *Aeneid* by Virgil to which so many allusions are made in the landscape garden, making it a kind of open-air classical theme park where visitors can learn about the ancients. Ceres had the sacred day of 21 December in common with Hercules in the Roman calendar, and thus at Stourhead the Temple of Hercules (now called the Pantheon) can be seen from the Temple of Ceres (Flora). Henry Hoare shared his grief for the loss of several relatives by building a temple to Ceres, who also suffered grief at the loss of her daughter, Proserpina. It was at the Temple of Ceres that Aeneas arrived, expecting to meet his wife, Creusa, but where he discovered that she had been spirited away to the underworld. Thus, he too was devastated by grief.

The contents of the temple's single room include a copy of the Borghese Vase with a relief of Bacchanalian rites. There are two busts representing Marcus Aurelius and possibly one of Alexander the Great, and in circular niches at either side of the room are marble female busts. The wooden seats are replicas of *pulvinaria*, which, at times of sacrifice, were placed near altars on which the ancients laid images of their gods in their temples. Now the Temple of Flora is used as a changing room at the time of the Fête Champêtre and the plays that are performed in front of the lake and delight thousands of people each summer.

The Grotto (1747–48)

Sometimes called the Temple of the Nymph, or the Nymphaeum due to the statue of Ariadne that lies asleep on a bed above a small pool, the Grotto is an inspired creation and a monumental work. Coming from the direction of the Temple of Flora/Ceres, a rock arch announces our arrival, through which we proceed to a pedimented entrance on which is the following inscription:

Intus aquae dulces, vivoque sedilia saxo, Nypharum Domus
Within, fresh water and seats in the living rock, the home of the nymphs

Here Virgil is describing the cave in the haven near Carthage where Aeneas and his men took refuge from a storm.

There is a small entrance chamber before we enter the main chamber, which is circular and about 6 metres high, with a similar width. There are four niches on either side of the pool, where candles would have been placed to light the grotto at night. Who would have been capable of such a feat of construction? In the absence of concrete proof, the likelihood is that Joseph Lane (1717–84) played a major part, being a local man from Tisbury, not far from Chilmark, where William Privett, Hoare's clerk of works, lived. Lane had also built similar grottoes facing water at Fonthill and Painshill in Surrey, where Charles Hamilton, a friend of Henry Hoare, created his own Elysium. He was one of few men of the time who would have had the skills to complete such a large chamber and its adjoining tunnels.

At the level of the surface of the lake, the main chamber has an opening in the rock that looks out towards the church in the distance. An oculus or skylight illuminates the central chamber, which was built mainly of brick and covered in flint and tufa, but which boasts little decoration, such as shell work. The floor is laid out with pebbles in a concentric pattern. At the back of the chamber lies a statue of a sleeping nymph reclining on her bed, from which cascades water into a pool. Sculpted by John Cheere, it is lead painted white. She is a copy of the statue of Ariadne, or possibly Daphne, the original of which can be found in the Belvedere Gardens in the Vatican. The latter was once thought to represent Cleopatra because of the snake bracelet around her wrist, but the Stourhead copy is without one, hence Horace Walpole's comment that she was like 'Cleopatra without the asp'.

In front of her and carved into the marble rim of the pool is Alexander Pope's translation of a pseudo-classical poem of the fifteenth century:

Nymph of the Grot these sacred springs I keep
And to the murmur of these waters sleep
Ah! spare my slumbers, gently tread the cave
And drink in silence, or in silence lave.

River God's Cave (1747–48)

To the side of the main grotto is the River God's Cave, wherein stands John Cheere's statue of painted lead, dating from 1751. The god, who was supposed to send the nymphs down the Stour to the sea at Christchurch, has his right hand outstretched as if he might have a trident as Neptune would have. The Swedish artist Fredrik Magnus Piper drew him with an oar in his right hand, but whether this is accurate is open to doubt as attempts to fit such an item there have failed.

It could be that the figure is holding his hand aloft in grief, without there ever having been anything in it, like Peneus grieving for his daughter, Daphne, who had escaped the advance of Apollo by being turned into a laurel bush, examples of which were planted above the grotto. Or is the River God simply pointing towards the path that leads to the Pantheon? His resemblance to the figure of Tiber engraving by Salvator Rosa, which has nothing in his hand either, confirms this view.

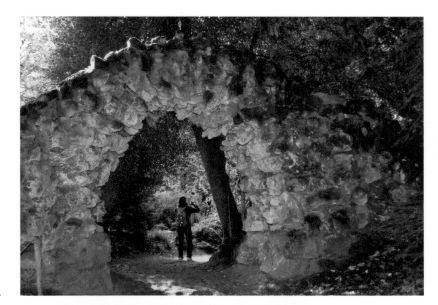

The Grotto Arch.

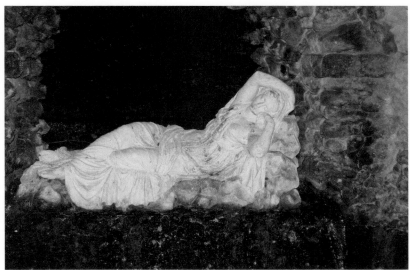

The Grotto
Nymph.

Gothic or Rustic Cottage (1780s)

This charming building with typical windows first appears on the estate map of 1785. The Gothic porch and seat were added in front of the very decorative bay window in 1806 by Henry Hoare's grandson, Sir Richard Coat Hoare. Francis Nicholson's early nineteenth-century painting shows it thatched and covered by a creeper, now replaced. It was converted into a summerhouse in 1895 and reroofed with stone tiles. Now it has the air of a Hansel and Gretel house, or a rather superior summerhouse with typically Gothic pointed windows.

The Pantheon or Temple of Hercules (1753–54)

36 feet in diameter and lighted from the cupola, the Pantheon was unusual for a garden temple in that it was heated for the comfort of visitors who wished to stay a while – a wise measure in the environs of a damp lake and with a collection of classical statues to preserve. Regrettably, the stove that provided the warmth has been removed.

Henry Flitcroft's most striking work in the landscape garden, it was originally called the Temple of Hercules to celebrate Michael Rysbrack's statue of the beefy classical figure. Before one enters the sacred chamber, one passes beneath the Corinthian hexastyle portico, to either side of which are two gods of pleasure, probably sculpted by John Cheere: to the right in a niche is Bacchus, god of merriment and wine, while to the left is Venus Callipygos, saucily lifting her robe to reveal

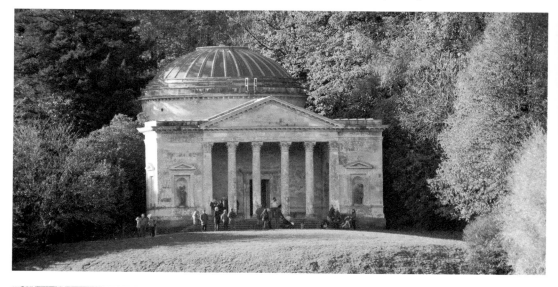

Above: The Pantheon.

Left: The Pantheon.

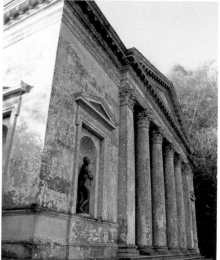

her buttocks, as if to entice the opposite sex. As a man of high morals, John Wesley 'could not admire the images of devils, nor should mankind reconcile statues with nudities either to common sense or to common decency'.

Inside, the decoration is very fine, with swags of grapes and scenes of festivities, yet its history is tinged with sorrow, with the much-bereaved Henry Hoare choosing to remember his late second wife, Susan. Set in a series of niches, the series of sculptures is probably the best in Wiltshire, demonstrating the finest craft and artistic merit. Henry Hoare wrote to his daughter, Susanna: 'I thought old Rysbrack would have wept for joy to see his offspring placed to such advantage. He thinks it impossible for such a space to have more magnificence in it and striking awe than he found here.'

In an anticlockwise direction from Hercules, the statues are placed as follows: Flora; Diana, goddess of hunting; and the Roman Saint Susanna, a reminder of his wife, Susan, and daughter, Susanna. In a clockwise direction are: Livia Augusta, who was the wife of Augustus Caesar and who is depicted as Ceres; the Greek hero Meleager; and Isis, an Egyptian deity worshipped as the ideal mother and wife, as well as the patroness of nature and magic. To depict the themes of marriage, birth, sport and death, Hoare commissioned eight bas relief panels of painted plaster made by Benjamin Carter to be installed high on the walls. Standing on the floor are seats whose backs were painted with classical scenes by William Hoare – a prominent society painter of Bath, but of no relation of Henry.

Like an Italian Renaissance casino where games were often played, it is close in spirit to Palladio's villas in the Veneto, built to remind the Grand Tourists, as Hoare was once, of the original in Rome. While there is much statuary to admire in those two places in Italy, there are few more noble statues of Hercules in England than the Stourhead version: his acceptance was immediate thanks to landscaper William Shenstone's poem and Handel's oratorio *Hercules*.

The Rock-Work Bridge (1762–65)

This has elements of a grotto with its apparent haphazard piling of stones, arches and various niches.

One enters through an arch of stones, and ascends by way of steps flanked by a series of rockeries and niches which generally contain nothing apart from one with a bench for sitting and admiring the view. The structure curves over the road to Zeals. A visitor, Joseph Spence, declared at the time: 'An odd sort of ruinous building which hides the road; and over which you wind by roughish steps, towards the Walk of the Muses and the Temple of Apollo.' The structure provides an element of the grotesque and the rude in contrast to the finery elsewhere.

The Temple of Apollo or the Sun (1765)

The inspirations for the Temple of Apollo are uncertain: some say that Flitcroft may have been inspired by an illustration in Robert Wood's book *The Ruins of Balbec*, a major archaeological site in Syria which was known as Heliopolis or the City of the Sun, whereby the Stourhead temple derives its name. Others say that Flitcroft may have taken ideas from the circular temple at Tivoli in Italy, but he never went on the Grand Tour as he came from a humble background. It is more likely that he saw William Chambers' Temple of the Sun at Kew, which had been built four years earlier, and was not far from where he was based in London. The Temple of Apollo/Sun was built

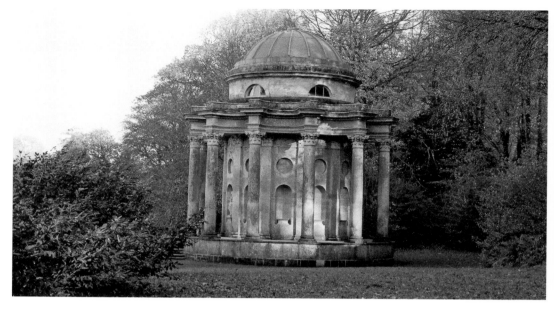

The Temple of Apollo.

in 1765 with 'detached' Corinthian columns according to architectural terminology, which means that they do not support any significant masonry but are connected to the main body of the structure by means of projecting masonry. Nine of the eleven niches around the outside are bare but two contain female statues, one holding an orb. The others have been removed to the house.

Inside stands a large cast of the Belvedere Apollo, which is lit from above by a skylight in the cupola – a roof which has been replaced several times, most recently to reduce it from a height that did not comply with the classical orders of architecture. In the coving of one part of the interior of the dome a dazzling plaster representation of the sun's rays has been created, thereby giving the temple its alternative name, and reminding the visitor that he had left the underworld and was once more in the light. Another of Hoare's *coups de génie* was to align the temple with the obelisk across the valley, with its Mithra, or sun disk, thereby reinforcing his iconographic message.

The Obelisk (replaced 1839–40)

As earlier indicated, this shaft of Bath stone is visible from the Temple of Apollo, with which it shares a solar theme. Obelisks were Egyptian symbols of the sun's rays and were revived in Europe as ornaments or memorials, in this case to Henry Hoare by his grandson Sir Richard Colt Hoare. A plaque with a dedication was added to the original obelisk, which was constructed by William Privett in 1746 on an avenue to the west of the house, but this fell into decay. The concluding words of the inscription say the following in Latin:

> The obelisk, which is an example of ancient obelisk extant in Rome,
> was constructed by Sir Richard Colt Hoare himself,
> nephew and heir, gratefully dedicated in the year 1815

The obelisk referred to is said to be the same proportions as the one at the Porta del Popolo in Rome. Here, its gilded sun disc sits gloriously on the top.

The Convent (1760s)

Tucked away in Stourhead Forest to the north of the landscape garden, this picturesque cottage has four odd-shaped obelisk-like pinnacles jutting out of the roof, which are made substantially of tufa. Thatched and encrusted with flint and random rubble, it has a rustic appearance. Once part of Stourhead's gardens, it acquired its name from the legend of a prioress who lived in this place and the twelve painted panels of nuns which once decorated niches in the drawing room. In Henry Hoare's time, there was reputedly a picnic cook who dressed up as a 'prioress' for the amusement of his guests, but the truth is that the Convent never served any religious purpose. By the 1980s, the house had fallen into ruins when architect Christopher Bowerbank bought it and restored it – at a cost of £50,000. He preserved many of the old features of the house, such as the gothic windows, and added a few of his own which complement them; for example, the pinnacles have been copied in the form of staircase lamps inside the house.

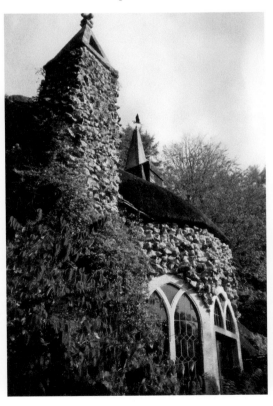 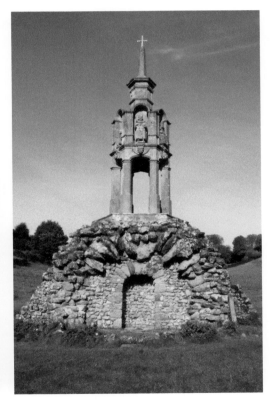

Above left: The Convent.

Above right: Saint Peter's Pump.

St Peter's Pump (originally built 1474, re-erected 1768)

At the same time as the Dean of Bristol Cathedral allowed Henry Hoare to remover the Bristol High Cross, he let the fragments of this curiosity go too. Originally built by Bishop William Canynges in 1474, this so-called 'castellette' stood over Saint Edith's Well, next to St Peter's Church, which gave its name. Now it can be found after a walk of more than a mile from the landscape garden near the top of a narrow valley called Six Wells Bottom, marking the highest spring from which the water flows down to the lake.

The bulk of the building is made of random rubble with a rough stone arch, the former pump superstructure consisting of six columns supporting a hexagonal canopy under which somewhat defaced statues of six clerics sit. Above them, an obelisk rises to about 10 metres. At ground level, a small hole where the water rises is surrounded by a pebble floor, and rough-cut stones point towards the centre of the arch. At the back, a large arch vaults over a bare wall.

Alfred's Tower (1765–72)

Designed by Henry Flitcroft again, it is one of the tallest folly towers in Britain at 160 feet or 50 metres high. Its situation could not be more prominent on Kingsettle Hill in a clearing in the extensive Stourhead Forest, and it is visible for miles around. It is said that Henry Hoare wanted

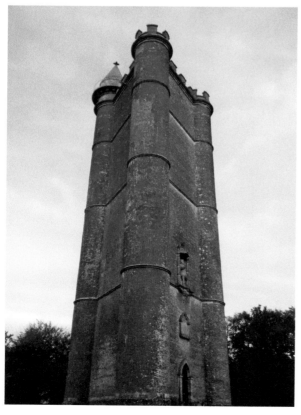

Alfred's Tower.

to replicate the campanile of Saint Mark's in Venice, but changed his mind upon reading the exploits of King Alfred. The taste for the Gothic was long-lasting, and for the English this also included Saxon, so Alfred chimed with this taste, especially as he was regarded as a symbol of British liberty.

After originally wanting to build the tower of stone, it was built with millions of bricks, and perhaps it was the search for any suitable material which delayed the construction. In the end, we have a design that is monotonously red, a far cry from Flitcroft's works around Stourhead's garden. It rises bleak and windowless, with just a few staircase slits to light your way to the top. It has round projections at each corner running all the way to the top, and one section of lighter coloured brick betrays an accident when a plane crashed into the tower. As for Alfred, his statue is a little in the style of a medieval relic and stands about forty feet off the ground on the east side.

The inscription beneath him, composed by Lord Bruce, says:

ALFRED THE GREAT
AD 879 on this Summit
Erected his Standard
Against the Danish Invaders
To him We owe The Origin of Juries
The Establishment of a Militia
The Creation of a Naval Force
ALFRED the Light of a Benighted Age
was a Philosopher and a Christian
The Father of his People
The Founder of the English
MONARCHY and LIBERTY

Stourhead once had a series of other follies and ornaments, mainly around the lake circuit, but time took its toll on these sometimes flimsy structures, including a Chinese Bridge, Turkish Tent, Chinese Alcove, Gothic Greenhouse, the Temple on the Terrace, Chinese Ombrello, a Statue of Apollo and a Hermitage. Henry Hoare also planned a minaret on a small island in the middle of the lake. Richard Colt Hoare, a serious antiquarian, could not stand such variety, so he had some of them demolished in the 1790s. He wanted to keep a predominantly Grecian look to the gardens, and found their heterogeneous nature distasteful. We know they existed not just from correspondence of the time but also from the paintings, sketches and drawings of various artists including the Swede Fredrick Piper and the Somerset landowner Copplestone Warre Bampfylde, who also created a folly garden at Hestercombe in Somerset.

Swindon

OS Ref: SU 116864; Postcode: SN5 5EX

In the twentieth century the oriental influence in Europe was principally culinary, and from the catering endeavours of the Chinese the Hongxin Restaurant, originally the Chinese Experience, was built in Swindon. From bland suburbia, one enters an exotic world through the highly decorated gate that takes the hungry diner to what is claimed to be the largest Chinese restaurant

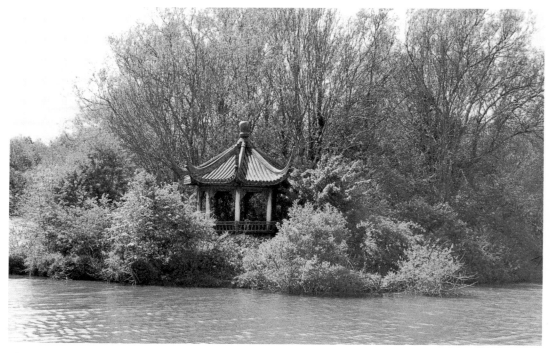

The Hongxin Restaurant Pagoda.

in Europe, half the size of a football field. Very much in the Chinese vernacular style, the building transports you to an exotic, far away world.

Designed by Devizes architects The Wyvern Partnership, the restaurant owes its existence in part to the liberal planning policies of the local authority – the Thamesdown Borough Council, as Swindon was known until the 1990s – which made development easy in this part of the M4 corridor. The restaurant was the brainchild of local people of Chinese ancestry, who reached back to their roots for authenticity in design. Led by Laurence Lee, this group of friends formed a limited company called Arttaste specifically to build the restaurant. They approached the council to rent land and found the development manager, Ken Hislop, sympathetic to their plans as he had spent some of the Second World War in the Far East, where he took delight in oriental architecture.

Lee declared: 'The project got bigger than we expected from our original quarter million pound investment, out of our reach, so we needed financial support, and I asked friends and relatives for money, as well as National Westminster Bank.' By the time it opened in 1990, the project had cost £2.06 million – more than eight times the original funding that Lee had envisaged.

Despite the enormous cost, Lee reminisced:

The restaurant looked like a funny building, and to make it look more oriental we employed the China Palace Art and Painting Company, a Taiwanese company with an agent in London. They put on the trimmings and decorations, like the panels on the walls, both inside and outside, the fish and other figures in the roof, and the inscription on the gate. They also put the white dragons in front of the main door, supposedly to keep evil spirits away.

The restaurant owners also employed the same company to design and build what is more of a fancy than the restaurant – the Pagoda. This charming building is squat compared to some pagodas, standing on a small island in a lake. It cost £30,000 but was worth it, for it blends perfectly into its setting, adding embellishment to the scene. Lee was glad that he abandoned the plan for a bridge to the island, fearful of the maintenance costs and the all-too-easy access for vandals in a spot a couple of hundred metres from the restaurant.

The pagoda was built of some very untraditional materials, such as fibreglass for the roof and a steel frame, thus giving it a better chance of survival than if it had been entirely made of wood. It was manufactured and painted entirely in Taiwan before shipment, only needing assembly and touching up of the paintwork on site. Nailin Yeh, head of the China Palace Art & Painting Company's European operations, says: 'It is a typical pagoda in the old Chinese style, with a roof curving up at the corners. In the old days it was popular to build one in the grounds of mansion houses for dinner and entertainment.' The restaurant building and its complementary pagoda form one of those scenes that lacks only a bamboo grove to make it look straight out of the Willow Pattern dinner service. Perhaps the Hingxin Restaurant should be preserving the scene on their own plates.

Teffont Evias

OS Ref ST 991312; Postcode SP3 5QY

There's nothing to connect the two towers in the grounds of the Manor House at Teffont Evias, a quiet parish in the valley of the Nadder, west of Wilton. Although the Manor House originated in the late Tudor period, much was added in a more Gothic style by John Mayne in the early nineteenth century, including the battlemented porch. Among the accretions were the two towers,

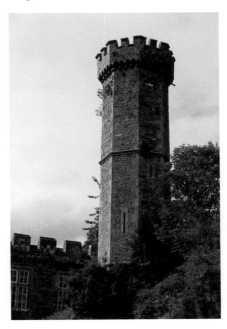

Teffont Evias' Water Tower.

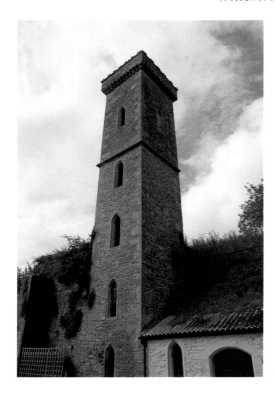

Teffont Evias' Hay Tower.

both standing tall, the first being the hexagonal Water Tower on the side of the house and on a rise. Attached to the house by a crenelated curtain wall, it is a high vantage point from which fireworks used to be lit during lavish Boxing Day parties given to the villagers. It is made of rubble stone in five stages, with double-chamfered pointed lancets to each stage, a hollow-moulded string course to the upper stage and a battlemented parapet. The arms of the Mayne family are in a quatrefoil above the doorway. Attached to the right is a single-storey outbuilding with five chamfered elliptical-arched doorways and five pointed lancets.

At the back of the house and attached to the rear wing facing a courtyard is the Hay Tower, this time square in plan and in five stages, with pointed lights and quatrefoils, a battlemented parapet with corbels beneath. There is apparently no door to this tower, and the openings on each stage are very small, and so one wonders how access is obtained. The answer is at the back: it is open at the top, which faces a field at a higher level, and was evidently used for agricultural purposes such as the storage of hay.

Tollard Royal

Several around OS Ref: ST 944170; Postcode SP5 5PT

The Larmer Tree Gardens lie at one of the highest points of Cranborne Chase, an unspoilt stretch of natural beauty that was once one of the great hunting grounds of the kingdom. In the time of King John it was especially active, for he lived and held court in the house now occupied by the owners of the estate in the village of Tollard Royal. The huntsmen met at the Larmer Tree, another name for a wych elm, marking the boundary between three parishes and two counties. Larmer was probably a corruption of 'lavermere', an incoming boundary in Anglo-Saxon, and now a new tree has grown up through the rotting bark of the old one. A small pyramid nearby commemorates the meeting of the hunt.

Centuries passed before Lieutenant General Augustus Lane Fox unexpectedly inherited the estate from his cousin in 1880. Already hailed as the father of modern archaeology for his innovative techniques, to inherit the estate he had to take the name Pitt Rivers, but took on much more: with philanthropic zeal he transformed the grounds around the Larmer Tree into a place of education, leisure and entertainment. This was the first private garden in Britain to be opened for public enjoyment. To persuade the general public to come and enjoy this little wonder was easier than one might expect in the days before cars, perhaps because it was completely free of charge and the story soon got about that a good time was to be had. To make access easier, a four-in-hand coach drove the 25 miles from Bournemouth every day – a fair trek more than a century ago.

The general was concerned with the education of the masses, but his conscience also told him that he was lucky to have all this wealth, and so felt an obligation to share it. His expenditure on the gardens was phenomenal, as scores of entries in the account books testify.

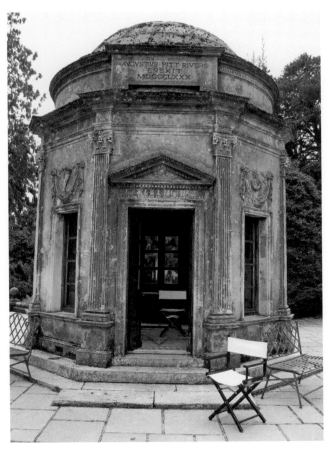

The Temple at the Larmer Tree Gardens.

For example, his extravagance extended to spend £18,500 in eleven years on trees, and £13 6s 0d one year on Peruvian bat guano, which was needed to fertilise the many plants in this Eden. In 1887 there were 15,351 visitors and by 1899 these numbers had grown to 44,417. The whimsical names of the picnic huts reflected the sort of animals that the general kept in the garden: Owls, Cats, Yaks, Stags, Hogs, Hounds, the Vista and Band View. The last of these was a reference to the bandstand, where a private band of estate workmen played. Trained by a professional bandmaster to keep up standards, they also wore an elaborate and expensive uniform.

Some of the buildings decayed, but more long-lasting was the Temple, a good example of an octagon, the first of the garden buildings erected by the general. The inscription above the north door tells us in Latin that he did so in 1880. The Temple stands about 12 feet high, and the exterior walls, which have now become impregnated with red lichen, rise in two steps and rejoice in a rich variety of decorative stonework, including Corinthian pilasters forming the corners of the octagon, before reaching a thin cornice which forms a break before the next level, slightly set back, reaching another thin cornice before becoming a shallow dome. The two doors have small, shallow pediments above them, and the four windows have decorative swags. Inside, there is a variety of decoration, including a frieze with swags, a mantelpiece, a maze pattern in the mosaics on the floor, a cast-iron grate and a bust of the general. The Temple marks a break between the lawn and the sunken garden, and a long flight of steps falls from the Temple towards the sunken garden and the Grotto – a plain cave made of massive stone, which contains a statue of Neptune standing on a fish with a trident in his hand.

The rest of the buildings mainly came in the later 1880s and '90s, but not all of them are extant, having collapsed through neglect. The survivors include the General's Room, which the general was reputed to have bought at the Earls Court Colonial Exhibition of 1897 and re-erected in 1899. Perhaps more accurate is the belief that he designed it himself and had it built by the estate carpenters, before then putting carvings from the exhibition on the façade. Whatever the case, this very attractive building has elaborately carved dark wooden canopies and deep eaves to the roof supported by heavily carved brackets. The window surrounds are particularly ornate, and inside the walls are lined with carved wooden panels.

The general's aim was to illustrate an unfamiliar culture to the masses, but it is likely that as soon as they arrived they made straight for the entertainments or horse races, which were held on the adjacent field. The other re-erection in the same North Indian or Nepalese style is the Lower Indian Room (1897). Much bigger and made of similar gloriously carved timber with lathe and plaster panels, it has carved doors and canopies. It also has glazed windows used for viewing the entertainments, as well as finely carved shutters and a veranda at the back. Its deep eaves are supported by heavily carved brackets.

The Singing Theatre (1895) is a magnificent wooden structure with wide Corinthian columns and a backcloth depicting ancient Greece. The acoustics are still perfect, and it was from here that on many a Sunday afternoon in the heyday of the park that one could see a group called the Kentucky Minstrels, as well as ventriloquists, conjurors and Punch and Judy shows for the children.

The first Wednesday in September was the biggest event of the year, with some 12,000 Vauxhall lights being used to light such popular events as the evening dance. Leading off the dancing on that magical night in 1895 was the poet and novelist Thomas Hardy. Lady Agnes Grove, a relative of the general, inspired him to write a poem on her death in 1926, reflecting on the night they first met:

CONCERNING AGNES

I am stopped from hoping what I hoped before
Yes, many a time!
To dance with that fair woman yet once more
As in the prime
Of August, when the wide-faced moon looked through
The bough at the faery lamps of the Larmer Avenue
I could not, though I should wish, have over again
That old romance,
And sit apart in the shade as we sat then
After the dance
The while I held her hand, and, to the booms
Of contrabassos, feet still pulsed from the distant rooms

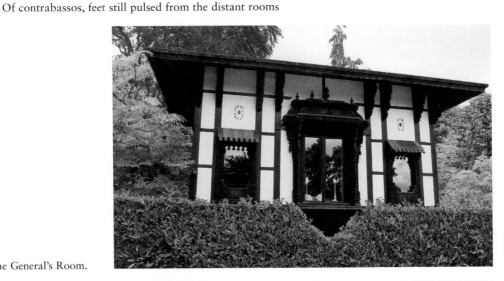

The General's Room.

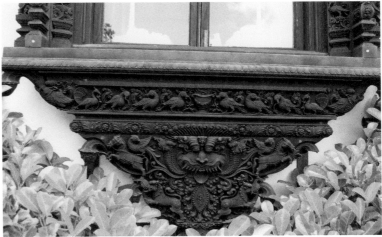

A wooden panel on
the façade of the
General's Room.

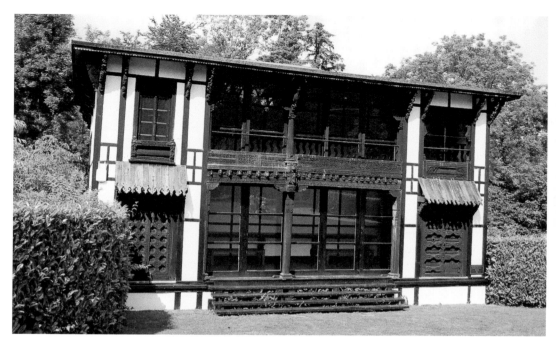

The Lower Indian Room.

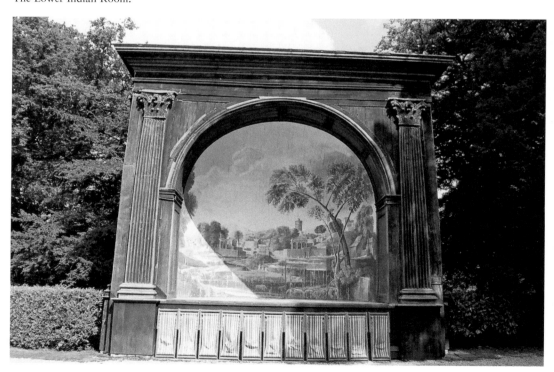

The Singing Theatre.

In contrast with the refined sentiments of this poem, it was a cruel night for Hardy, for he suffered a stiff leg and never danced again.

The Larmer Tree Gardens are part of the vast Rushmore Estate, which owns various tracts of land in the area amounting to 7,500 acres. Rushmore House stands at the centre of a large deer park and was the home of the Rivers and later the Pitt Rivers from the early nineteenth century, until it became Sandroyd School in 1939. At the edge of the cricket field stands the Temple of Vesta. It was built in 1890 by the general at the considerable cost of £1,792 to commemorate the birth of his first grandson. It is said to be similar to the temple that the general saw at Bramham Park. Here, a perfect rotunda set on a six-stepped plinth and consisting of eighteen fluted columns of Bath stone. The columns have a golden hue and are topped with Corinthian capitals and surmounted by a low dome made of copper.

Later the Pitt-Rivers family moved into King John's House and built a Japanese Pavilion and complimentary garden, from where an allée leading through the woods can be seen. Until 2008 it lacked a final 'stop' to the view; something which would crown the estate. William Gronow-Davies, the inheritor of the estate from Michael Pitt-Rivers, decided that the view needed finishing off and started to negotiate with the telephone network O_2 for five masts to be incorporated into a structure at the top of the hill, where they would be visible from King John's House. The local authority planners decided that the need for new mobile phone

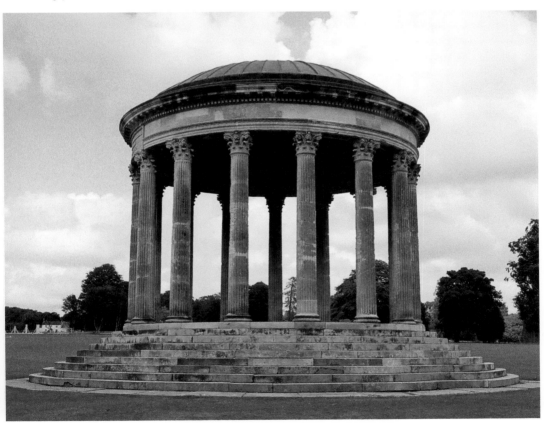

The Temple of Vesta at Rushmore House.

aerials outweighed conservation concerns and gave the green light to the Indian Moghal Arch. However, when the mobile phone company pulled out of the deal, Mr Gronow-Davis was undeterred and decided to go ahead all the same with the proposed folly as it still had valid planning permission.

Situated just inside Dorset, it stands 56 feet high, is four-sided and is rendered in cream and orange. It has four chattris, or domes, with wide eaves supported on narrow columns, one on each corner, and between them all is a central dome, built slightly higher. Each has a gilded spire piercing two small globes at the bottom. The chattris sit on chajjas – projecting eaves which form part of the roof – and the inscription 'WJGD 2008' on the west side records its creator and year of construction. The architects were Walshe Associates of Worcester, who made it of concrete rendered in lime, and sections of the four pillars were washed in red ochre lime. The base is made out of Turkish limestone and includes the Pitt-Rivers crest, along with the four points of the compass. Its five copper domes are still capable of housing any aerials in case a telephone company should wish to avail themselves of such a striking, high-placed structure.

Trowbridge

OS Ref: ST 853578; Postcode BA14 8HR

Built incongruously in Bythesea Road, Trowbridge, the Pumpkin Tower came about partly through corporate neglect and partly through the opportunism of local businessman Tom Rothschild, who was best known for his Elm Tree Reclamation Company in Westbury Industrial Estate. Allied Dunbar, the new owners of the Shires Shopping Centre, removed a huge, rather ugly but powerful clock tower, which they did not wish to maintain. As if to compensate, Rothschild, who lived opposite, managed to somehow get planning permission to build this strange edifice at a cost of £80,000.

It is a 45-foot-high round tower jutting out of the pitched roof of a relatively low building in the town centre. A sewer pipe, normally used horizontally, was turned vertically and then clad in stone and other decorative features that Rothschild had reclaimed through his business. These include four openings on its street side: the lowest two are small rectangular windows, followed by a very small circular window with a cross-shaped window frame and then a larger circular opening near the top. It is surmounted by a pyramidal roof with a small cross on top, though the building clearly does not bear the faintest resemblance to a church.

It used to be known as the Millennium Tower, though it was clearly not typical of the projects that people were accustomed to at the time, which elsewhere tended to bring some public benefit such as sporting or entertainment facilities. Nonetheless, to celebrate Millennium Night in 2000, much jollity was to be had when its dragon gargoyle was reported to belch out fire and smoke.

When built, the Pumpkin Tower – as it is now known for no apparent reason – created quite a stir in the town, with letters and lampoons appearing in the local media. But did the locals have an ambiguity towards it? One correspondent seems to herald it as 'an immense benefit for the town as Trowbridge will rank among the top 10 tourist attractions of Great Britain', but then he says they would see 'the biggest and most hideous folly in the United Kingdom'. Another correspondent exclaimed: 'What is Trowbridge coming to? It is like something out of the Dark Ages. Even from a horror movie! The council's central area committee all want firing. What were

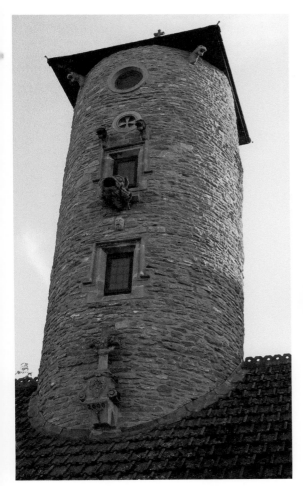

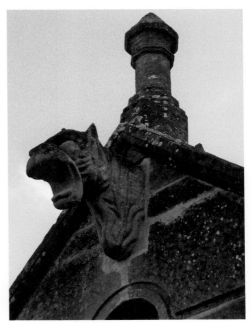

Left: The Pumpkin Tower.

Above: A gargoyle on the Pumpkin Tower.

they thinking of?' Another was more upbeat: 'Individual, eccentric and architecturally perverse, the tower is without doubt the most exciting building erected in Trowbridge this century ... Trowbridge lost its sense of humour around the time of the Black Death. I think Mr Rothschild's folly goes some way to restoring it.'

Despite its uncertain merits, it gained approval among at least some of the burghers of Trowbridge by winning a Special Certificate at the Trowbridge Millennium Dinner. After a brief period as employment agency offices, it has reverted to residential use.

Wardour Castle
OS Ref: SU 939263; Postcode SP3 6RR

In a secluded valley near Ansty stands the impressive bastion of Old Wardour Castle, almost impregnable since its building in the fourteenth century. However, ruination came in the Civil

War, after which it almost acquired the aspect of a landscape feature, but a chance was missed of making it into an eyecatcher when later generations of building were added to the estate. The main chance was when the 8th Earl of Arundell built his New Wardour Castle, much further up the valley and out of sight, to the designs of James Paine from 1770 and with landscaping by Richard Woods.

Despite the limitation placed on his plans, Woods' association with Wardour appears to have been long and fruitful, for the Banqueting House, sometimes called the Gothic Dining Pavilion, was probably of his design but may have been executed by Capability Brown in the 1790, some twenty years after Brown started his own landscaping. The building has crenellations, stained glass and an ogee door, window frames and panels, and an interior with the original marble fireplace

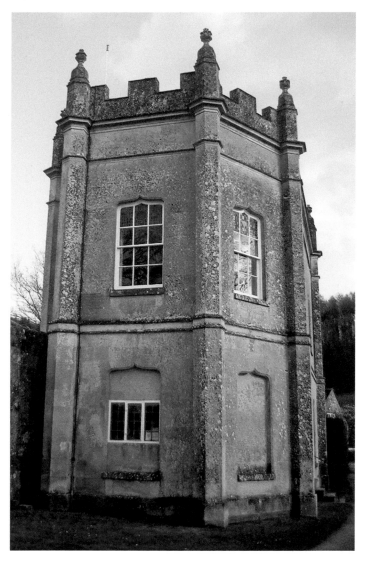

The Banqueting House at
Wardour Castle

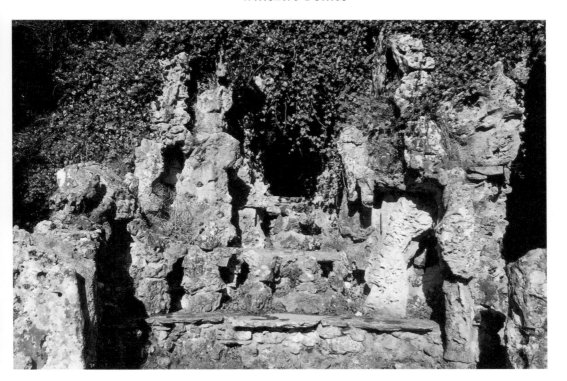

The Wardour Castle Grotto.

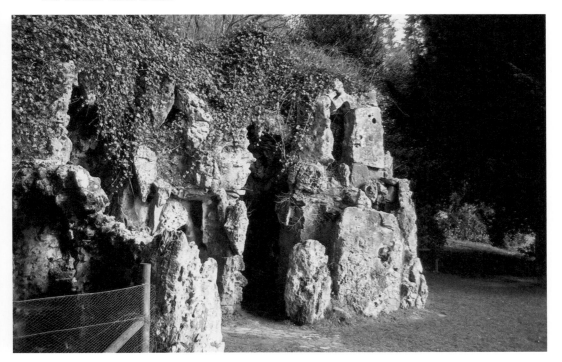

and window shutters. Rutter, in his *An Historical and Descriptive Sketch of Wardour Castle and Demesne, Wilts*, describes it as: 'A spacious apartment ... on the chimney pieces are several of the cannon balls that have been found since the siege, with other curiosities. The north-west windows afford a pleasing view of the fishponds and surrounding park etc.'

On the other side of the old castle bailey is the Grotto, a fantasia of tufa rockwork entirely set above ground, approached by steps from the court lawn. Executed in 1792 reputedly by Josiah Lane, the son of Joseph, who set up the family grotto-building business in nearby Tisbury, its ragged edges and irregular shapes give this corner of the park a rococo feel. 20 feet high, its long shape and limited interior is not typical of the Lanes' style, who generally went in for rounder shapes that accommodated at least one room. There is little use of ammonite or minerals, tufa being the predominant material. The pinnacles and towers of the grotto may have been created to mirror the ruins of the castle. Inside, tunnels twist and wind, leading nowhere in particular. Seats invite the curious to pause and contemplate, and the whole is made gloomier by yews, which hang over the grotto.

Westbury

OS Ref ST 885508; Postcode BA13 3ED

Hanging on the western edge of Salisbury Plain with fine views into Somerset, a rare example of a Chinese garden has been created at Beggar's Knoll. Since 2000 the current owners, Colin Little and Penny Stirling, have infused the place with their Sinophile tastes, having visited China numerous times in order to soak up the atmosphere of the country's green spaces, and on a visit to Vancouver in 1999 they were inspired by the Dr Sun Yat Sen Garden. They draw on Chinese philosophy and thinking, saying that the main purposes of a Chinese garden are relaxation, enjoying plants, taking in the scenery and admiring the architecture.

One enters the Garden of 10,000 Shadows through a gateway and sees a Buddha well ensconced among the planting. A sign in Chinese says 'Friendship with Foreign Devils', as if to suggest that the spirits of the garden can make peace with the natives who come into this very exotic place. One can sit in the Harvesting the Moon Pavilion, which is a play on words in the Wiltshire legend of the Moonrakers, who harnessed the moon in their smuggling endeavours. When the Revenue men were after them, they 'raked' the moon off a pond in which they had thrown their pursuers. Like many Chinese houses, the corners of the pavilion are turned up to keep the demons away, making it harder for them to enter, and the zigzags in the adjacent paths prevent the demons from catching you as they can only run straight.

One enters the Three Friends of Winter Garden through a brightly coloured gateway with a carved dragon on its façade (the symbol of the Emperor) and a phoenix (the symbol of the Empress). Many Chinese gardens were made by 'scholars' or others who had retired from official jobs, and in the Scholar's Garden there is an attractive seat and a sculpture of a fat man who represents prosperity.

Set high above the drive stands the Wildly Cheering Pavilion, which celebrates the local council's abandonment of a bypass proposed for Westbury that would have cut in front of Beggar's Knoll. The translation of the Chinese proverb says 'Everything grows well in the garden'. Further up at the top of this blessed plot is the Bamboo Garden, with appropriate planting, and the Bamboo Pavilion, which has a carving of five bats on the ceiling. The word for bat in mandarin is '*foo*'.

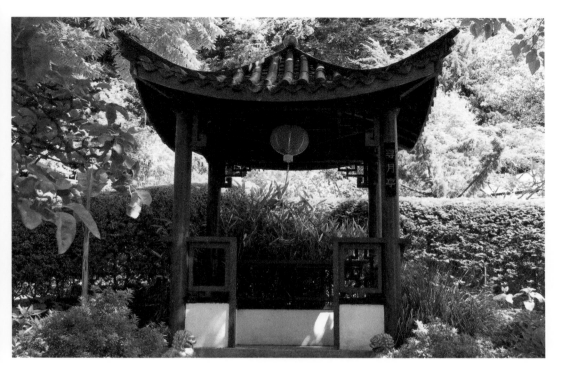

Above: The Harvesting the Moon Pavilion.

Right: The Wildly Cheering Pavilion.

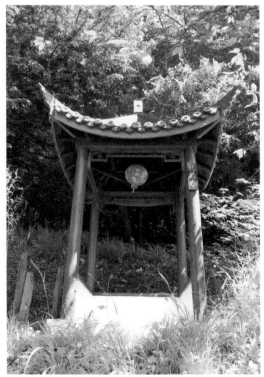

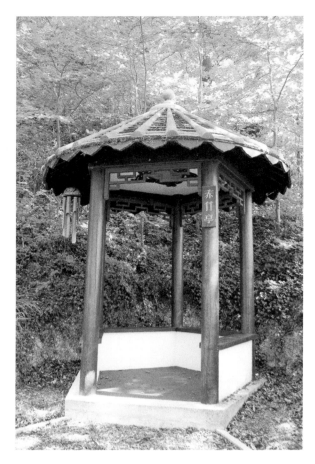

The Bamboo Pavilion.

This is also the word for 'good luck', but it is said with a different tone, so this building plays on this linguistic feature. The Chinese characters on the outside mean 'Raising the Bamboo Pavilion', the word for pavilion being '*ting*' – a word found in other Chinese buildings in British gardens.

Whiteparish

OS Ref: SU 212248

The Pepperbox was one of the very first gazebos to be built in Britain, in 1606, and despite the passage of more than four centuries little has been passed down about its origins. Standing in an isolated situation south-east of Salisbury on Brickworth Down, near the A36, the Pepperbox has the look of a garden gazebo that has lost its garden and the house attached to it. It was built by Giles Eyre of Brickworth House, after whom it is also called Eyre's Folly, probably as a hunting stand, for it lies on a down with a view typical of buildings put up for that purpose.

According to Peter and Jean Hansell in *Doves and Dovecotes*, it was used as a dovecote more recently, and while it is typical of the dovecote style, no niches to make pigeons feel at home are

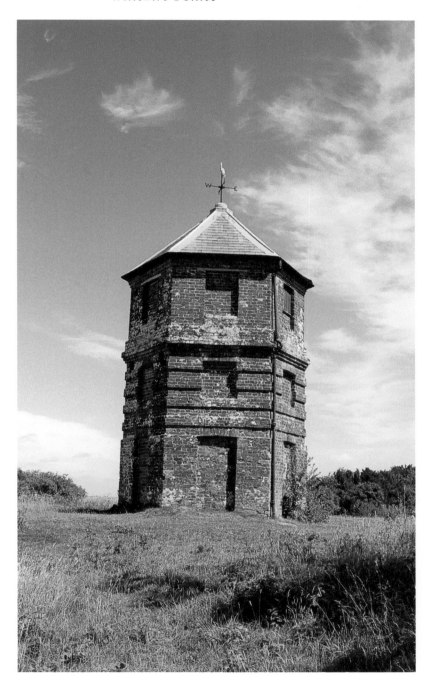

The Pepperbox.

visible from the outside. Hexagonal and around 10 metres high, it is almost totally redbrick to the point of dullness, made duller for the number of bricked up windows and arches, but relieved by a slate-tiled pyramidal roof and weathervane.

Much of what we know of Giles Eyre can be gathered from the slightly cryptic inscription on his tomb in Whiteparish Church:

> Buried here Giles Eyr Esq and Jane his wife. A man
> much oppressed by publick power for his laudable
> opposition to the measures taken in the Reigns of
> James and Charles the first. In the year 1640 (for then
> well known Court Reasons) He was **** afterwards
> plundered at Brickworth by the King's soldiers of 2000[1]
> value and imprisoned for refusing to pay the Sum of 400[1]
> demanded of him by two instruments under the privy seal
> bearing the date at Oxford 14th Feb 1643. He was Bapt: Feb
> 1572 and dyed Jan: 1655 having issue 7 sons (3 of whom were
> likewise members of Parliament) and 4 daughters.

Thus it seems Eyre was a member of parliament at a time when it is likely he sided with the Parliamentarians if one takes accounts of his privations, and three of his sons followed in his footsteps. The four stars in the inscription appear to replace a deleted word and the superscript number 1 only means pounds in respect of the sums demanded of him.

There may be some justification for its alternative name of Eyre's Folly for when Sir Thomas Gorges built the unusual triangular-shaped Longford Castle in the valley below him, it is likely that Eyre felt that he was not to be upstaged, and had to give the semblance of superiority by building a look-out tower.

Wilton

OS Ref: SU 096309; Postcode: SP2 0BJ

The story of Wilton's follies is almost as turbulent as its gardens: some have been swept away, others have been moved, and one has been cannibalised into something completely different from its original form. The seventeenth-century Wiltshire writer, natural philosopher and antiquary John Aubrey declared that: 'This curious seat of Wilton and the adjacent country is an Arcadian place and a paradise.' He was referring to Sir Philip Sidney's prose work *Arcadia*, which draws heavily on this part of the county, but soon the garden was to be changed drastically by Philip Herbert, the 4th Earl of Pembroke, with the creation of a rigid and formal garden in the French style. Among the features was the Grotto House, the exceptionally elaborate and complex creation of Isaac de Caus, son or nephew (lack of any birth registers at the time means we cannot be sure) of Salomon de Caus, who was an authority on hydraulics, as shown in his *Les Raisons des Forces Mouvantes*. The Grotto House was situated in the centre of a balustraded walk at the end of the long central avenue that led from the house – the object of many visitors' perambulations around the feature-full grounds.

Isaac de Caus's grotto was the talk of high society and the engineering impressed all who saw it too: the hydraulics were powered by means of a stream which flowed through the kitchen garden, turning an engine that raised the water into a cistern. The Grotto House was brimming with statues, including spouting sea monsters and other ornaments, and was ingenious in its

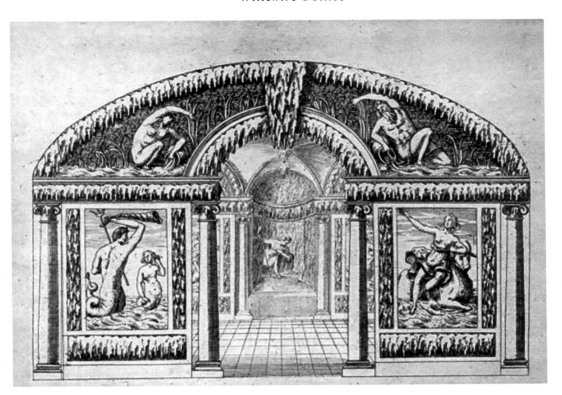

Isaac de Caus's design for the Grotto in *The Gardens of Wilton*, published *c.* 1645.

flow of water, including a rarity in England – *giocchi d'acqua* (or water jokes), which sprayed visitors with water unexpectedly. The Grotto House cost the 4th Earl some £10,000, a very large sum for him considering it was a third of his annual income, from which he had to support 120 family members.

Alas, Henry Herbert, the so-called Architect Earl, 'destroyed the old ridiculous water works and whims' and some major parts of the Grotto House were re-erected to form the façade of the Park School House. Originally built as a school for the estate children in 1838, it is out of the public gaze in a corner of the garden as a private house which incorporates the front of de Caus's grotto – and what an explosion of carving it is! A feast for the eyes – a 'tour de force ... in grotesquerie' according to the architectural historian Christopher Hussey – there are many features including putti, or representations of children, scantily clad and in a variety of expressive poses: 'deranged goblins' according to Timothy Mowl. The foliage carving is especially ornate, like a riot of curves and twists.

The 9th Earl was an amateur architect who admired the work of Andrea Palladio so much that he supposedly took one of the Italian architect's unexecuted designs for the Rialto Bridge in Venice, and turned it into something particularly suited to the English landscape garden, the Palladian Bridge. It is likely that the 9th Earl relied heavily on his clerk of works, Roger Morris, to flesh out his ideas. The date cut in the masonry is 1737, and the initials 'I. D.' also appear, which record that John Devall was the mason-sculptor who did most of the physical work – for £103.

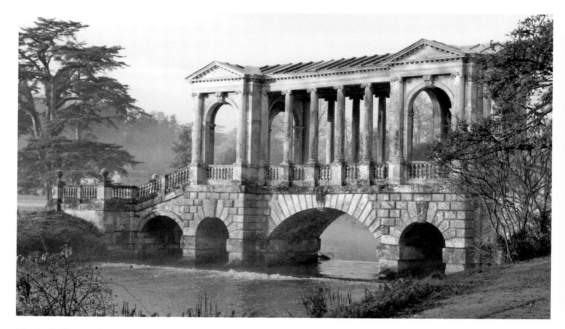

The Palladian Bridge.

A genuine prototype, the bridge was copied at Stowe and Prior Park and it quickly became the talking point of fashionable visitors. Let one John Loveday of Caversham take us over it:

> ... tis a very light and most elegant Structure upon 5 rustic arches; besides the beauty of it, this building serves two uses, that of a foot-bridge and that of a Summerhouse on both sides of the Water. You ascend the bridge by wide Stone Steps at the foot of which is a handsome Approach of Stone; the building is of the Ionic Order, under such an Arch you enter a square room, passed which you are in an oblong Space supported on each side by four Ionic pillars, not Arches; at the other End of this Space is another Square room.

The view from the bridge originally had the Triumphal Arch as an eyecatcher on top of the facing hill, which was built to a design executed early in the career of William Chambers around 1760. The arch is crowned with the equestrian statue of Roman Emperor and philosopher Marcus Aurelius with his right arm outstretched. Probably copied from an original statue in Rome, it was executed in the Restoration period of the 1660s. Like so much of Wilton's architecture it did not stay there long, for James Wyatt brought the arch and statue down close to the house, and made it form the entrance to the front courtyard of the house, adding small lodges to either side.

Still standing on the same hill is the Casino or Casina, which is also an eyecatcher from the house. Built around 1759 by Sir William Chambers, it has a tetrastyle Tuscan portico with a pediment on a rusticated base, which contains the servants' quarters, including a kitchen. This would have made it an agreeable banqueting house or gambling den out of earshot of the house. Access to the upper salon is by balustraded staircases either side, and it once had a stuccoed and plastered finish but this has been eaten away by damp. Now, red lichen is growing on the Chilmark stone.

The Holbein Porch is another removal. Originally an entrance to the Great Hall of the sixteenth-century house, it dates from around 1560. Now standing next to some tall trees to the west of the garden, it was wrongly attributed by John Aubrey to Hans Holbein, who was more famous as a painter of royalty and aristocracy than architecture. As with the Triumphal Arch, James Wyatt did the removal job in around 1800. It's a curious piece with short Ionic columns below and Corinthian columns above, both fluted and reeded. On top there are coupled fan pediments in the shape of shells supporting mythological beasts. Each façade has coats of arms in the centre and two busts on either side in roundels. Open entrances are on three sides, leading to an interior which has some fine mouldings decorating a rather dank tunnel-shaped vault.

Wilton has impressed many people, not least a certain J. Warton, who wrote a sonnet entitled *After Seeing Wilton House* in bad doggerel, but with recognition that follies can contain a certain stylistic mimicry:

From Pembroke's princely dome, where mimic art
Decks with a magic hand the dazzling bow'rs ...

Bibliography

Books

Bannerman, Isabel and Julian Bannerman, *Landscape of Dreams* (London: Pimpernel Press, 2016).

Batey, Mavis and David Lambert, *The English Garden Tour* (London: John Murray, 1990).

Bevington, Michael, 'Henry Hoa re and the Creation of His 'Demy Paradise', *Studies in Iconography*, Vol. 12 (1988).

Bold, John and John Reeves, *Wilton House and English Palladianism: Some Wiltshire Houses* (London, Her Majesty's Stationery Office, 1988).

Britton, John, *The Beauties of Wiltshire*, (London: Vernor, Hood, Wheble & Britton, 1801).

Britton, John, *The Natural History of Wiltshire* (1847).

Châtel, Laurent, 'The Mole, the Bat and The Fairy, or the Sublime Grottoes of "Fonthill Splendens"', *The Beckford Journal* Vol. 5 (1999) pp. 53–74.

Colt Hoare, Richard, *The History of Modern Wiltshire* (London: John Bowyer Nichols, 1829).

Headley, Gwyn and Wim Meulenkamp, *Follies, Grottoes and Garden Buildings* (London: Aurum Press, 1999).

Hull, Margaret and Gerald Hull, *Half-Forgotten: The Grotto Work of Joseph Lane (1717–1784) and his son Josiah (1753–1833)* (Bath: Private Publication, 2017).

Jones, Barbara, *Follies & Grottoes* (2nd Edition) (London: Constable, 1974).

Mowl, Timothy and Brian Earnshaw, *Trumpet at a Distant Gate: The Lodge as a Prelude to the Country House* (London: Waterstone, 1985).

Mowl, Timothy, *Historic Gardens of Wiltshire* (Stroud: Tempus Publishing, 2004).

Pevsner, Nikolaus: The Buildings of England. Wiltshire (2nd Edition) (Harmondsworth: Penguin, 1975).

Rutter, John, *An Historical and Descriptive Sketch of Wardour Castle and Demesne, Wilts* (Shaftesbury: J. Rutter, 1822).

Symes, Michael, *The English Rococo Garden* (Princes Risborough: Shire Publications, 1991).

Thacker, Christopher, *Masters of the Grotto – Joseph & Joseph Lane* (Tisbury: Compton Press, 1978).

Thompson, Michael, *General Pitt Rivers: Evolution and Archaeology in the Nineteenth Century* (Bradford-on-Avon: Moonraker Press, 1977).

Woodbridge, Kenneth, *The Stourhead Landscape* (The National Trust, 1989).

Websites

British Listed Buildings at www.britishlistedbuildings.co.uk

International Grotto Directory at http://thespasdirectory.com

Parks and Gardens UK at www.parksandgardens.org